DRAWING
INTO PRAYER

A 30 Day Prayer Guide into His Presence
for Personal, Family, and Small Groups

Christian Moore

Copyright © 2014

All rights reserved.

DEDICATION

To My Wife Gosia

To Dad

To My Praying Mother

To My Spiritual Father Carl H. Stevens

To My Pastor & Example Thomas Schaller

A Special Thanks to:

Trish Watson & Melissa Quickel
for their patience in editing
&
Sebastian Palmeri for the excellent cover artwork

TABLE OF CONTENTS

The Genesis of a New Creation in You

Before we could approach the subject of prayer in this small book, we are prompted to evaluate the natural state of every human being, and that being unregenerate, spiritually dead, impotent. A man that has been seeded from the earth, born of the flesh, is therefore flesh. We originally being fleshly and blind to the things that of the Heavenlies, are in need of new "genesis" in the deepest part of ourselves. That "genesis" differs from the Biblical account of the origins of the material world in that it has an entirely different source. "That which is born of the flesh is flesh, and that which is born of the Spirit is spirit." - John 3:6. This source afore mentioned is rooted in the Heavenlies and shares nothing with the soil we stand on now. The Source from which this comes is from The Spirit of God Himself.

Mankind needs a total rebirth, an absolute rejuvenation that is sourced from that Heavenly sphere from which springs up a new creature. Mankind cannot be remade, remodeled, or refashioned. You and I need a new genesis - a creation that is not made from the materials from ourselves, or this world.

God created this universe not out of mandate but out of love, and because of love God sends His only Son into it to rescue it. Jesus's love and mission to this world was terminated by the ingratitude and sin of man (and of you and I). Yet it was the Love of the Spirit of God for humankind that raised Jesus from the dead and burst Him from the sullied grave.

Thus we may be reborn by this Love from Above. Anyone that allows the Love of the Spirit of the Father to enter and believe on His Son that He sent, will be a recipient of a supernatural miracle - a rebirth of the Spirit of God. Something or rather better stated; Someone will be born inside that is born from Above, that is sourced from Above, and speaks the language of Above.

This is the new creation that the Bible speaks so much of. This new creation is born of the Spirit and cannot sin, fail or be destroyed. It is sourced from the Seed of the Gospel of Grace. Just as a new born babe cries out for it's mother's breast and her caress, so this new creation hungers and thirsts for God; His Word, His Love and His Communication to the inner most parts of who we are.

If you have not received Jesus Christ as your Lord and Savior, do so now. Believe on Him today as your Forgiver from sin and your Guarantor of Eternal Salvation. The peace of God will flood your soul as you trust Him in surrender. You will witness the genesis of a brand new miracle YOU.

This is beginning of prayer.

ABOUT THIS BOOK

My prayer is that the Spirit of Intercession and Pleading would breathe on this little book and draw you into God's presence to enjoy deep communion with Him and clarity of direction in your Prayer Life.

I am not in anyway claiming to know how to pray, but like you, am a disciple, as those who long ago inquired of the Great High Priest - "teach us to pray."

The content of this book is comprised of sermon notes preached here and overseas, hand scribbled notations in my Bible, meditations, quotes, stories of old, illuminations by the Spirit of Prayer, many table conversations, and from hours and minutes in His presence.

As you read this little book, surrender to the gentle voice of the Spirit leading you into His presence and discover the most satisfying, fulfilling era of your life as a Christian.

"The potency of prayer hath subdued the strength of fire; it had bridled the rage of lions, hushed the anarchy to rest, extinguished wars, appeased the elements, expelled demons, burst the chains of death, expanded the gates of heaven, assuaged diseases, repelled frauds, rescued cities from destruction, stayed the sun in its course, and arrested the progress of the thunderbolt. Prayer is an all-efficient panoply, a treasure undiminished, a mine which is never exhausted, a sky unobscured by clouds, a heaven unruffled by the storm. It is the root, the fountain, the mother of a thousand blessings." - Chrysostom

I. THE SECRET OF PRAYER

"I am the Almighty God - Walk before me" - Genesis 17:1

"O, let the place of secret prayer become to me the most beloved spot on earth." - Andrew Murray

There is a great secret that many believers never discover in their Christian lives - a joy and a privilege that remains hidden to many. Hidden not because of its exclusivity or selectiveness, nor because of the inability to attain to it, but because of its narrowness, a gate that is as the eye of a needle. It is a way that demands the stripping of all worldly baggage even to the loss of our love for self.

In return, there is an ushering into the presence of the Almighty, a surrender to His Love and a healing realignment of our dislocated soul to it's place under the governance of the Spirit of the Word.

When we get quiet before the Holy One in surrender, and the soul hushes it's tantrums, we can hear the Still

Small Voice whispering, "Come unto me all that labor and that are heavy laden..."

This is the secret of the all satisfying communion with the Creator of our soul - PRAYER.

DAY 1
TURNING ASIDE

"Now Moses kept -- the flock of Jethro his father- in-law, the priest of Midian: and he led -- the flock to the backside of the desert, and came to the mountain of God, even to Horeb. And the angel of the Lord appeared unto him in a flame of fire out of the midst of a bush:and he looked, and, behold, the bush burned with fire, and the bush was not consumed. And Moses said, I will now turn aside, and see this great -- sight, why the bush is not burnt. And when the Lord saw that he turned aside to see, God called unto him out of the midst of the bush, and said, Moses, Moses. And he said, Here am I." - Exodus 3:1-4

"When Christ calls a man, he bids him come and die."
- Dietrich Bonhoeffer

This verse marks the condition of much of Christianity today; many believers meandering in the desert alone, occupied with meaningless duty, lost to true purpose, and struggling with inner frustration and dismay. Yet this is where God brought Moses, forty years later after his rout in Egypt, to a people that were not his own, in a wilderness far from home, and to a family that he did not come from. He was a lost man.

God allowed the utter failure of Moses in Egypt to work out of Moses all of himself; his own confidence, cleverness, and personal determination. It was vital for Moses to be emptied of himself and it took forty years for that to be accomplished.

Now it is done, and Moses is ready, though he does not yet know it. That day, Moses walked in the direction of Horeb, the mountain of God, whether he knew where he was going or not, the Ancient of Days, the God of the Hebrews, His God, was to meet him there.

While journeying, a burning bush caught his eye. Burning bushes were not uncommon there at the edge of the desert, but this one was, for it burned without the bush itself perishing. His hunger for the mystery of the supernatural, more than his curiosity caused him to exclaim; "I will now turn aside, and see this great sight, why the bush is not burnt." What Moses saw was mystery, a secret, an anomaly that foreshadowed his own future calling.

As he turned aside, God called him, from the midst of the bush, from the core of the flame in the midst of the frail sage -

"Moses, Moses"

God called out to Moses, and Moses simply replied, "Here am I" - there was not much more to say than that. Moses was where he was and who he was; there were no excuses, no explanations, no hiding, only honesty.

"Draw not nigh hither: put off thy shoes from off thy feet, for the place whereon thou standest -- is holy ground." Moses was not to draw near and examine the phenomenon with his trained mind from the courts of Pharaoh, but he was to remove his shoes and stand barefoot on the rocky terrain that now had become Holy. He was to only listen and sense the impression of the Holiness of God's presence on the most sensitive part - the soles of his feet - in his very familiar environment.

What Moses saw was a picture of himself - the All Passionate Flame of the Spirit of God burning within his delicate human frame, consuming all within, save the frame itself.

Friends, today there is the call of that same God on the mundane life where we've been lost to our purpose in a foreign land. This is where we see the Spirit of Burning engulf the weak structure of a mortal.

God must do it this way because the "way of a man is not within himself" - Jeremiah 10:23. We must be brought as Moses was, to the edge of the desert for a great emptying of ourselves that we ourselves cannot initiate or control. It may be long, arduous, and painful process. But in the end we will not be consumed, but purged of all of ourselves, a vessel prepared by God to be filled by that flame of God for His purpose. It is then we find ourselves, outside of ourselves, immersed in the call of the Holy One.

The way into communion and prayer begins with a great sense of being lost to ourselves, lost to our purpose, out of control, and a feeling of being off balance. More often than not, intimacy with God at His mountain begins at the end of a road of much failure and frustration. There we are alone, empty of our self and all its issues, and ready to see, turn aside, and hear in holiness.

This is where the way begins.

DAY 2
SHUT THE DOOR

"But thou, when thou prayest, enter into thy closet, and when thou hast shut thy door, pray to thy Father which is in secret; and thy Father which seeth in secret shall reward thee openly." - Matthew 6:6

"Do not have as your motive the desire to be known as a praying man. Get an inner chamber in which to pray where no one knows you are praying, shut the door, and talk to God in secret." - Oswald Chambers

When the disciples petitioned our Savior how "to pray" Jesus preempted his response by saying "when you pray, enter into your secluded place and when you have shut the door, pray."   Jesus addresses our location and separation.

The "closet" is our choice of a refuge, away from the commotion of people, work, family, duties, and the clamor of the daily grind. There is much to be gained in learning how to be still, "study to be quiet" the apostle tells the Thessalonian church - 1 Thessalonians 4:11. This is a lost art that has caused a diseased society, hyperactive in its mayhem.

The shutting of the door is significant in the Bible as we see many times. The prophet Elijah shut the door behind him and the dead boy before he prayed and the boy was revived. Jesus shut the door with three of his disciples before raising the lifeless child. A shut door connotes separation and concentration, without which there cannot be communion and an ensuing miracle.

Sadly, it can be that prayer is never fully enjoyed due to a lack of consecration. Where there is no shutting of the door in consecration, there can be no concentration. Consecration cannot begin where there are the ramblings of psychic noise that arise from a restless soul; a soul that has not met his God before a simple burning bush in the remote parts of his desert.

When in your prayer closet, with the door closed and in a position that is comfortable, open your Bible to a Psalm or a passage of Scripture that is meaningful to you, that stirs your heart and spirit. Read it slowly,

quietly thinking about each word. Stop at a word that penetrates you and mull it over in your heart repeating it at times until it penetrates. This is what the Psalmist spoke of in Psalm 39:3 "My heart was hot within me, while I was musing the fire burned." If stray thoughts interrupt or urgent prayer requests come to mind, then don't try to resolve them at the moment, the answer for them will come from the Spirit later, after you're quiet. Set them aside and return to your Scripture and reread it, getting back to your process of focus. This is true meditation - Joshua 1:8, 1 Timothy 4:15, not an abstract mantra of mindlessness, but rather
a focus on a Word, a Scripture, that in itself is life breathing and quickening.

This takes study and exercise. Studying to be quiet is a critical discipline of the learning child. Depending on the momentum and the pressures of your day this could take several minutes before a stillness pervades the room and the soul quiets. At this moment the soul has found its place in surrender before the presence of the Word.

Generally at this point, a streaming of God's thoughts and His mind begin to flood our weaned soul. Often times wisdom and answers come to us before we even pray for them from our prayer lists. You may notice instructions that come from God about ministering and resolutions to issues that have remained locked up. Once in this flow of prayer and hearing, there can be moments of worship and praise, or just a holy silence before the Almighty.

When we learn this discipline of solitude and separation, time, however long or short it is, is not the issue. The accomplishment is that the soul has found its place in the presence of its Creator and can be realigned to its proper place and be healed. When practiced everyday over a period of time you will notice a growing emotional stability, clarity of thought, discernment of spiritual things, and deep peace that prevails over stormy waves that flood the soul.

If this can be learned, then our soul takes its rightful place in harmony with the body under the governance of the Spirit, and Christ reigns over us with sweet communion.

DAY 3
INTIMACY BEFORE THE ALL-SEEING

"Thy Father which seeth in secret shall reward thee openly." - Matthew 6:6

"The yearning to know what cannot be known, to comprehend the incomprehensible, to touch and taste the unapproachable, arises from the image of God in the nature of man. Deep calleth unto deep, and though polluted and landlocked by the mighty disaster theologians call the Fall, the soul senses its origin and longs to return to its source." - A.W. Tozer

When the door has been shut and we are alone with God in surrender and in quiet, we then can be captivated by Him in communion. Yet the temptation is to begin to recite religious prayers or read through our prayer list as if God did not know or see what weighs on our hearts. We presume that we must say as much as we can to make sure God is aware of our plight and perplexities. We actually make God into our own making by projecting onto Him our unregenerate perception of Him. The result is our incessant speaking and rambling in prayer for however long we wish; then we get up, walk out of our prayer closet having fulfilled our religious rite for the day. Yet, in doing so, we have not been touched by His Comforter and there has been no true intimacy with the Lover of our Souls.

Thus the rebuke by Jesus to the Pharisees who were oblivious to intimacy with God. Their god was the shadow of Jesus rather than the person, a form but no exposure to His searching. Religion has no might but is blinded by itself, worshiping an intangible person. The Pharisees and the religious professionals of the day purposely had it so, due to their pride and unwillingness for true intimacy with God - because intimacy denotes exposure, the willingness to be "seen" through and through. The Pharisees would have nothing to do with that.

The Psalmist wrote, "Thou hast searched me and known me" - Psalm 139:1. God had searched out David's most inner secrets and yet God loved David. He searches us, exploring every hidden place locked up. When trials pass over us and heartaches prevail, He searches us out. When we soar in the exhilaration of joy, or sink into sullen despair; He knows our soul. "Thou hast know my soul in adversity" - Psalm 31:7

There can be no true prayer without intimacy. He needs no permission to know you and me deeply, yet what is needful is our admission to ourselves that He knows what we hide in shame from before His eyes. It is much like the father who embraces his fleeing son from the kitchen with a hidden cookie in his hands. The son in silence feels his father's hand touch the stolen cookie covered in hand. The son then knows two beautiful things; that his father knows of the cookie hidden and that his father loves him. No words were expressed but the effective truth has been known in a moment of intimacy in communion with the father. The truth being that it's more than just the cookie enclosed in the little hands but that omniscient love creates a bigger picture in intimacy.

The child of God can know this also. We are caught in His embrace in our prayer closet, feel the touch of the Hand of God on those hidden things and we are delivered from them in the silence of His grace and His loving knowledge of us.

DAY 4
PUT OFF THY SHOES

"And he said, Draw not nigh hither: put off thy shoes from off thy feet, for the place whereon thou standest -- is holy ground." - Exodus 3:5

"Prayer is weakness leaning on omnipotence." W. S. Bowd

"Draw not nigh thither" appears to be contradictory to the message of the new covenant, yet it stands as a prerequisite for communion for a mortal man, callous to the Beauties of Holiness. El Shaddai could not speak to Moses whilst his feet were shod with his sandals. For Moses to hear God's voice he must put off his shoes and stand bare footed on the foreign terrain of His presence. Shoes undoubtably represent today's fashion, pride, accomplishment, and selfish stance. They represent the fearless and sure-footedness in the injurious desert. It is commonly known among orthopedists that the sole of the foot is the most sensitive part of the body because it is where nerve receptors connect to every organ of the body. The Holy One desires our sensitivity to Him and His holy anointing in every part of our soul and body through attentiveness. This was mandated before Moses could come near to Him.

When humbling ourselves before the God of Horeb, our shoes are no longer donned and we can feel with our feet, the ground of God. We must tread on, walking circumspectly, not in unhealthy introspection, but endeavoring to walk before Him being diligent not to grieve his Holy Spirit.

Being set aside in seclusion within our prayer closets and learning to study to be quiet, we move on to exercising ourselves in sensitivity to the still small voice by removing our indifferent shoes in humility. God resists the pride of man's loquacious opinion.

Humbling ourselves is not necessarily a work we accomplish but an adjustment to our thinking. Humility has been once described as not thinking too highly or too lowly of yourself, but not thinking of yourself at all. That seems quite impossible in the self-oriented world we live in today where people are brain washed into orbiting themselves in their personal universes.

In prayer, we become lost in the person of God and His love, thus progressively become less and less aware of ourselves. This is what the apostle John meant when he said "He must increase and I decrease" - John 3:30. As God increases and our occupation with His wonderful nature intensifies, we are delivered from self-centeredness.

Prayer is the application of the heart to God, being delivered from ourselves and unto the voice of God who has something to say. Shedding our shoes of pride and our personal rights in the presence of the God of Horeb we become partakers of His plan.

DAY 5
THE BEAUTIES OF HOLINESS

"Hallowed be thy name." - Matthew 6:9

"Prayer - secret, fervent, believing prayer - lies at the root of all personal godliness." - William Carey

Many a saint has struggled with the deep sense of the lack of holiness in his life and the intense desire for consecration. It has burned like a fire in the recesses of their spirit like a flame - yet, alas, to no avail. Still they live in the humdrum of their daily life; indifferent to the things of God, with no urgency to pray.

I met a man once who told me while in the midst of his debauchery and helplessness of sin; "I used to pray that God would give me the desire, to just desire freedom and holiness." Paul cried out similarly in his lowest estate in Romans 7, "O wretched man that I am!" It seems that God must allow us to see our depravity and unbelief in its ugliest form for us to cry out in utter helplessness. Peter was there when he cried "save me Lord for I perish" as he sank into the dark waters he once triumphantly walked upon.

This moment of desperation when we finally cry out to God on our face before Him is that moment that we discover the beauties of God's holiness and His grace. We become illuminated to the hidden treasure of God's will - His way. As it was with Moses, so it is with you and me in prayer. We discover as we walk before His face that we are clay vessels, broken, unable to contain water as those vessels of Jeremiah 2:13. The first thing we see is our unworthiness and our heart's cry is "Who am I?"

That question is always answered by God in the same way each and every time any man of God has asked it in the Bible. It is answered by these words - "I AM". Like Moses, our self-absorption of unworthiness is quickly swallowed up in His holiness, His person.

In Isaiah 6, when it was his moment of intrepidation before the Ancient of Days, God sent an angel to take a burning coal from off the eternal altar of the sacrifice to cleanse Isaiah's unclean lips. After that, Isaiah discovered the beauties of His holiness and he said in absolute yielding, "here am I send me!".

We will often feel the unworthiness that accompanies our fallen flesh, and we will be tempted to strive in His presence in prayer for acceptance. We will be tempted to modify the act of prayer into a cleansing program or a system of attainment to higher heights with God. Whenever we think of heights or attainment we are already off the rails and heading down the path of self-righteousness. Holiness is not an attainment or accomplishment; it is a gift given to the sinner by His grace. It is the effect of the Holy One touching the unholy.

O' this is the Beauty of His Holiness! Not by our own works of righteousness that we have done! This is what Moses met at that flaming bush! His unworthiness overwhelmed by the worthiness of the loving I AM that was sending him back to his country where he had utterly failed. Sent in return to be an instrument in the hands of God.

When the broken man comes to the Cross, he discovers a secret that no arrogant man can see or know. It is that flowing Blood that drips upon the sinner's brow and purges him from all his sin!

Our work is but to bow our head and let Him cleanse us. In our prayer closet we must first behold the beauties of His holiness, lest our prayer be striving to ascend a ladder of endeavoring that would be no different than building a tower of Babel to meet the Heavenly.

DAY 6
THE HEART-PRAYER

"Our Father which art in heaven, Hallowed be thy name." - Matthew 6:9

"In prayer it is better to have a heart without words than words without a heart." - John Bunyan

It is of no mistake that the disciple's prayer in Matthew 6 begins with "Our Father, who art in heaven." It is a petition that begins first with relationship, and that of family, not servant-worker to master. For it is relationship that is the underlying characteristic of prayer; prayer is encompassed in the sphere of our spiritual family - Ephesians 3:14 - "For this cause I bow my knees unto the Father of our Lord Jesus Christ, Of whom the whole family in heaven and earth is named."

David, that sweet shepherd after God's own heart wrote "God setteth the solitary in families" - Psalm 68:6. It is in the affectionate family of God that we discover the joys of prayer. Prayer is a communion of belonging when we were once solitary.

It is with the spirit of adoption that we cry out to our new found Father, "Abba!". When we do not know how to even pray as we ought we have an Intercessor, the Spirit of the Father, that intercedes for us according to the will of God - Romans 8:26. What child is there that does not know the yearnings within, that naturally cries out to his father when he is frightened or burdened? Does not the child know the inclination he has for where he belongs at supper time or where his bed is when he is far from home? To be a son is to know the love of the Father, for in love there is no barring of communication however honest and forthright it is.

Prayer therefore is prefaced by the unconditional security of a family that validates its relationship. This is where it begins; it begins from the heart. The new heart of Ezekiel 36:26, the heart that is a heart tuned to discern the voice of its father - Jeremiah 24:7.

Prayer is more heart than it is intellect. Though the mind is engaged in prayer, it is subservient to the new heart from God. The new heart sets the precedent of relationship for our minds. Thus the promise, Hebrews 8:10, "For this is the covenant that I will make with the house of Israel after those days, saith the Lord; I will put my laws into their mind, and write them in their hearts: and I will be to them a God, and they shall be to me a people."

True prayer is simply the application of the heart to God. It becomes as involuntary as breathing. This is prayer mentioned without ceasing in 1 Thessalonians 5:17. The heart beats and we draw air and exhale it. As we speak with the very air we exhale - so goes prayer, we breathe in the love of the Father and we exhale prayer in words formed by the life giving love of God our Father. Prayer begins the life cycle of respiration for the beloved child of God. We draw the air of the security of the Father's love and we exhale praise, worship; we exhale song and His Word. Prayer may be just as silent as breathing in the quiet adoration of our Heavenly Father. Prayer is not the rambling of heartless words from a prayer book or hymnal, but prayer is the raptured breath of an awed saint captured in the love of his Father.

Simply put, our prayers are to be the words we breathe out to the Father from our very heart that beats. Prayer is not prayer until we understand that it is our life breath. If prayer is so, then it is inclusive of the intermittent expression of groanings that cannot be uttered from a saint's burdened heart or a child's broken heart. What beautiful untranslatable language is a child's rhythmic breath resting in its father's arms! So it is to be of our prayer.

The prayer of the heart to our heavenly Father is the prayer heard more than the rightness of religious head-prayer that has no unction, no cry, and no burden. All too often we go to prayer with what we ought to pray, without ever exposing the true burden of our hearts because we are not secure in the Father's love. Cry out to Him from your heart as the genuine honest shepherd did in his psalms - for the Psalmist had a heart after the Father.

DAY 7
THY WILL BE DONE

"Thy kingdom come. Thy will be done in earth, as it is in heaven." - Matthew 6:10

"Prayer is not overcoming God's reluctance, but laying hold of His willingness." - Martin Luther

The ultimate crucible of prayer was displayed in the Garden of Gethsemane, that moment when Jesus, with great drops of sweat and blood dripping from his brow, in prayer cried out, "nevertheless not my will, but thine, be done" - Luke 22:42. Prayer is not the persuasion of God to do our will or our wishing, but that we would, under the crux of the moment, capitulate to the Father's will.

The will of man shifts as the waves of the sea, changing like the wind, he does not know what he really needs. His need is pegged on the whims of what he feels he needs, which lacks all objectivity. These needs change with the wind.

Man does not know what he needs, he does not understand his own decrepit heart, he knows so little about himself, let alone how to pray. So in the act of prayer there must first be the voluntary, willing surrender of all to God's kingdom and His will.

Prayer, as yielding to God in quiet, is the progressive discovery of His will over our will. It is He that is increasing and we in turn, are decreasing. It is the magnification of God, His nature, His word through His Spirit till He becomes all in all. Therefore it is a process and a very long one indeed.

When the saint bends his knee in prayer and allows the Word to hush his noisome heart, the many voices of want and need fade at the audience of the Almighty. The saint then hears that still small voice that speaks His will.

The Spirit prays in our infirmity, our ignorance; for we do not know how to pray as it is proper and pertinent.

The Spirit prays not abstractly but "according to the will of God" - Romans 8:27. It is in that moment as Jesus prayed, "not my will be done but thine be done" that we discover the will of God in prayer. It is there we discover God's will.

Thus prayer is actually a stilling of ourselves, being united at His cross in God's mind through His Word in Spirit where He actually begins praying through us. Our prayers become prayers according to the will of God and not "asking amiss" as the apostle James said. We then, under the unction of the Spirit of God, bid of the Father that petition He has put in us to ask Him for; His Will is done on earth as it is in Heaven.

II. PREPARATION: THE DEEP CALLING TO THE DEEP

"Deep calleth unto deep" - Psalms 42:7a

"But God hath revealed them unto us by his Spirit:for the Spirit searcheth all things, yea, the deep things of God. For what man knoweth the things of a man, save the spirit of man which is in him? even so the things of God knoweth no man, but the Spirit of God." - 1 Corinthians 2:10-11

"God does not delay to hear our prayers because He has no mind to give; but that, by enlarging our desires, He may give us the more largely." - Anselm of Canterbury

DAY 8
THE NEED FOR INTIMACY

"In all their affliction he was afflicted, and the angel of his presence saved them: in his love and in his pity he redeemed them; and he bare them, and carried them all the days of old." - Isaiah 63:9

"When we sing, 'Draw me nearer, nearer, blessed Lord,' we are not thinking of the nearness of place, but of the nearness of relationship. It is for increasing degrees of awareness that we pray, for a more perfect consciousness of the divine presence. We need never shout across the spaces to an absent God. He is nearer than our own soul, closer than our most secret thoughts." - A.W. Tozer

We live in a fast paced world ever accelerating in information and shallow relationships. Yet people's need for intimacy is accentuated by the lack of real relationship, leaving many in a growing sense of loneliness. People have become more increasingly like isolated islands in the sea of humanity - talking and texting, but not being heard, hearing and not really understanding.

Society is comfortably accustomed to meet at an arid and hollow place to exchange something physical or even soulish while the unseen heart cries out for the intimate and meaningful.

The intimacy that we are craving for cannot be met at the physical plane only, nor at the soulish level. Our physical body is aware of people and the world we live in: its media, mentality, fashion, food, entertainment, news, career, and the such. Our soul is only self-conscious of its inner psychic noise of fear, shame, guilt and what it wants. The intimacy we were made for can only take place at the spiritual level- where the depths of the Spirit of God call out to the depths of the spirit of a person.

This is what Job was pleading for when he said "Even today is my complaint bitter: my stroke is heavier than my groaning. Oh that I knew where I might find him! That I might come even to his seat! I would order my cause before him, and fill my mouth with arguments. I would know the words which he would answer me, and understand what he would say unto me. Will he plead against me with his great power? No; but he would put strength in me. There the righteous might dispute with him; so should I be delivered forever" - Job 23:2-7.

Job wanted to be deeply known, deeply heard, deeply understood.

David yearned for this intimacy also in Psalm 42:7 when he said "deep calleth unto deep at the noise of thy waterspouts." The Hebrew word used here for "waterspouts" is sinnor which refers to a water shaft hollowed out of stone, a water tunnel. It describes water that flows through the tunnel suddenly and quickly, creating a rushing sound of turbulent water.

For there to be that intimacy that we so deeply desire, there must be first the drilling down through the stone of the physical world-consciousness, tunneling deeper still, through the soulish self-conscious, until there is the breaking through into that spirit inside of us. Then, and only then, can the refreshing waters from the depths of God's Person fill our thirsty soul, Psalm 42:1-2. This is that moment when His Spirit witnesses with our spirit that we belong, that we are not lost orphans, but sons and daughters. This relationship and nearness that we experience in prayer is a nearness that is closer to us than our very soul, our very memory, and our very breath. We can hear His whispers, He has no need to shout for He is closer to us than we are to ourselves. This is true intimacy. This is the sum of all that we need.

DAY 9
THE DRAWING

"No man can come to me, except the Father which hath sent me draw him" - John 6:44

"Prayer is the drawing and pressing of the impressed image toward its original, which is the Triune God." - Abraham Kuyper

It is all important that it be understood that the act of prayer originates from the Spirit of the Father drawing to seek Him in prayer and not our own will and endeavoring. There is nothing in mortal man that prays. He has no prayer in himself. Man ought to pray but the truth is he cannot, nor does he wish to see the value of prayer; for he does not even know what prayer is. Man is only aware of the world he lives in and what he wants for himself, by himself, because his spirit is unregenerate. Man is bound to himself and finite in his understanding, he is not seeing the Eternal. The carnal man, whether believing or not, lives only in the sphere of his own pain, joy, sin, and success. By himself, he cannot know anything outside of his limited sphere of senses, yet he is very aware of the cosmic loneliness within, not knowing how to inquire for the remedy.

The Bible's opening chapters show us God seeking and calling out to lost man, "Adam, where are you?" - Genesis 3:9. It is in this moment that God's compassion is stirred for man's blind plight trapped in fear. He begins to draw his fallen creation with bands of love, Hosea 11:4. This drawing is mystical and cannot be described by words, it is beautiful and attractive. It was the attractiveness of Jesus as He prayed in Luke 11:1 that drew his disciples to say, "teach us to pray."

It is that sweet Word from the Father Himself that speaks directly to the innermost tabernacle of a man saying, "Seek My Face." When our heart responds it says, "Thy Face will I seek," as David said in Psalm 27:8. We are drawn to God in a mutual desire for communion. It is to become our discipline to hear

His whisper "Seek My Face," just as we would tune our
ears to hear the cooing of the morning dove outside our window.

When there is no desire or urge to pray, do not try to will it, but do as the Shulamite as did, she mused on her lover and their previous engagement. She called for her beloved, "Draw me, we will run after thee" - Song of Solomon 1:4. She waited in her chambers in stillness, straining to hear her beloved's voice to call her out.

Prayer that is willed is not prayer. It can easily become a spiritless recital of heartless words. Prayer is to be the breathing out of love towards The One who draws us with bands of love. This kind of prayer is as easy as breathing because it's a prayer of the heart - the heart that God has given us to know Him, Jeremiah 24:7.

DAY 10
THE BREAKING DOWN OF THE
THREE WALLS
OF SEPARATION

"For He is [Himself] our peace... and has broken down (destroyed, abolished) the hostile dividing wall between us" - Ephesians 2.14

"Many and many a man is crying to God in vain, simply because of sin in his life. It may be some sin in the past that has been unconfessed and unjudged, it may be some sin in the present that is cherished, very likely is not even looked upon as sin, but there the sin is, hidden away somewhere in the heart or in the life" - R.A. Torrey

There are three walls that block the upward prayer of the saint. Number one is what the Scripture calls iniquity, a hidden rebellion or emotional reaction in the heart to the Will of God or His Word. The prophet Isaiah pointed out to Israel - "your iniquities have separated between you and your God" - Isaiah 59:2. A large number of Christians today may say "there is no sin in my life" but live with buried bitterness and disagreement to what The Planner has allowed in His will. When we secretly become bitter or wounded in the plan, it results in the breakdown of communion and fellowship with God. This kind of isolation is created when we react, feeling scandalized, rather than entering into His rest. Iniquity in the mind blocks the wisdom needed for the plan, the peace in the plan, and the grace for the plan. I remember when my mother passed away, that she had a handwritten note on her desk that said, "Can you trust me for the thing that I have allowed and not ask me why?" Those words speak very deeply to me and address that plaguing question we so often struggle with. When we choose to trust Him, we are no longer alienated. The wall of iniquity and all our "whys" become quiet praise - "Though he slay me, yet will I trust in him: but I will maintain mine own ways before him." - Job 13:15

The second wall that thwarts prayer is sin. The practice of sin or living in the memory of sin effectively stops prayer. No man can pray and sin simultaneously. One excludes the other. Not only does sin cause prayerlessness, prayerlessness always precedes sin. God has with a Word of finality dealt with your sin forever - John 19:30, "It is finished." Until we agree with that Word of finality about our sin, then that wall of silence shall stand unmovable

between us and God. But O' how sweet the communion of breaking the bread and
drinking the cup when we surrender our sin to the Sin-Bearer Jesus! How speedily we hear His voice and see His face!

The final, yet most obstinate, of the three walls is the wall of idol worship. The prophet Ezekiel described hidden chambers and cellars in the homes of many men in Israel where they secretly worshipped idols and images - Ezekiel 8:12. This happens today in the hidden rooms of believers' souls. Worship simply means the concentration of our attention, whether it's positive or negative. Any three-dimensional object or murky issue in our soul that steals our focus for any amount of time from the One that is our object of adoration is an idol. Technology, careers, noble endeavors, family, or inner fear, unforgiveness, bitterness, comparison, jealousy, even the ministry of serving God, have become idols in today's church.

The truth is that anytime Jesus is not the focus of our mind, body, and soul, then walls spring up causing a disconnect of fellowship with God. At that point we lack an understanding of who we are in Christ, and our eternal purpose.

In reality, the problem lies deeper than the concentration of our attention; it lies in the fact that when there is no consecration, there cannot be any focus. Consecration is experienced only when we surrender at the dusty foot of a splintery cross. There, our sins were judged and peace with God was made. Only there do we discover He who is our peace and that the three walls of separation have been broken down.

DAY 11
FORGIVENESS

"...because that the worshippers once purged should have had no more conscience of sins." - Hebrews 10.2

"To be a Christian means to forgive the inexcusable because God has forgiven the inexcusable in you." - C.S. Lewis

Though we approach this subject of forgiveness today, it takes a lifetime to implement, via daily applying the healing balm of Gilead. Forgiveness is the breath we inhale, prayer is the breath we exhale. Anything less is spiritual suffocation. Prayer is hindered when stubborn unforgiveness reigns.

Much has been written about the effect that unforgiveness has on the human body, the human psyche, and the quality of life. Forgiveness is vital to our life energy; it is not optional. We must forgive, and when we do, we are most like God. As we forgive, we ourselves are healed by the cleansing catharsis of God forgiveness - Luke 11:4a. Only then can we advance down the road of communion with The Master in prayer.

That brings us to turn our attention to two unresolved issues that must be addressed in a believer's life: forgiving ourselves and forgiving others.

Forgiving Ourselves: God has compassion on our sinful plight, seeing the dilemma of our helplessness. He is moved with compassion, John 3:16. Our "self-compassion" is not effective and only leads to self-pity and all the other complexes of self-consciousness. He remembers that we are made of dust and He knows our disposition in Psalm 103:14. Thus He was moved to act through the act of His Son's atoning work on the Cross.

Look at the vivid illustration of forgiveness by the "scapegoat" of Leviticus 16:20-28. The picture of the scapegoat is the transference of guilt and the offense of mental sin as well as the acts of sins. It is the bearing away of the presence of sins, removal of the consequence, separation from association and ownership of sins. At this moment we allow the Spirit to unveil our eyes to this truth. We realize we do not live in the presence of our sins any longer. This includes memories, by the fact that the scapegoat was to be sent into a "land uninhabited." This is to express the truth that to remember our sins and to morbidly lament over them is to be guilty of stealing, stealing something that has been taken from us and that no longer belongs to us!

Forgiving Others: People offend and hurt us not knowing fully what they are doing. We must begin with compassion for the perpetrators when we evaluate what people have done to hurt us. This is the first step in forgiving others. Most Christian psychologists agree that forgiveness begins when a victim that has been unjustly hurt or violated, willingly releases the painful debt owed by the offender for the purpose of healing both parties. The human conscience fashioned after the likeness of God requires payment for an offense. The offense cannot be brushed aside or ignored. The way the conscience is built is that it will quietly seek out resolution and justice until it is satisfied. Then it will rest. Again we refer back to Leviticus 16 as the principle of forgiveness in the Old Testament as best illustrated in verses 1-19. After the bullock was sacrificed for the debt of sins and its blood shed and sprinkled on the mercy seat for the consequence of sins, then, and only then, can the conscience be satisfied of payment for the violator's offense. How much more the Blood of Christ is effective over the blood of bulls and goats to wash us and sprinkle our conscience that demands recompense from others?

Let us examine Job who lost everything and then was accosted by his friends. As with Job, forgiveness comes full circle when the victimized, out of Godly compassion for the perpetrator, prays for them and for their blessing. Thus, when Job, at the end of his trial, prayed for his friends who were to blame for much hurt; the Lord kept back the punishment He had for them. Furthermore, He released Job from his captivity, restoring to him two-fold of what was lost in his calamity - Job 42.8,10. Perhaps Job's release was from the prison of unforgiveness toward his friends.

Forgiving others begins by agreeing with the Great Judge who declared forgiveness. Just agree with Him and confess "forgive them for they know not what they do!" When we do so by faith, the healing balm of Gilead begins to flow and we experience a sweetness of love that doesn't originate from us. It may not be that we completely forget what was done, but we are healed by the Love of God and we forget the pain and anger associated with it.Thus the unforgiveness, bitterness, and memory of the hurt of our's and others' sins begins to be healed. It is then that fragranced anointing begins to permeate our tabernacle as the communion with that Great Forgiver flows outward as living, forgiving, healing waters.

DAY 12
VULNERABLE TRANSPARENCY - AUTHENTIC PRAYER

"O Lord, you have searched me [thoroughly] and have known me. You know my downsitting and my uprising; you understand my thought afar off. You sift and search out my path and my lying down, and you are acquainted with all my ways. For there is not a word in my tongue [still unuttered], but, behold, O Lord, you know it altogether." - Psalm 139.1-4 (Amplified)

"...but all things are open and exposed, naked and defenseless to the eyes of him with whom we have to do." - Hebrews 4.13b (Amplified)

"Honesty and transparency make you vulnerable. Be honest and transparent anyway." - Mother Theresa

We have all entered headlong into prayer with our religious prayers, praying for what we "ought" to pray with our prayer lists, neglecting the cry of our heart or ignoring the issue that remains unconquered by God. We act as if God overlooks the closed and locked room in our soul that we hide so well: the pain, the sin, the pride, the uncomforted wound that all lie behind that guarded door.

We board up that door because that part of the soul has been functioning in infirmity for so long and we fear the pain of re-injury. As we pray our flowered prayers, God nods as it were, yet He is interested in that bolted door and yearns to enter in and heal it. As long as there is any neglected, hidden area of our soul, barred from surrender to the omniscience of God, there can be no true fulfillment of intimacy in prayer, but only shallow religiosity and loneliness.

We live in a world where permanent relationships have become passé and masked with a status quo exchange creating a generation of isolated and unreached people. Transparency before God in prayer is only possible when we become secure in the "safe zone" of God's Love. There, we can be sure we will not be hurt or forsaken as it may have been in our childhood or in a relationship in the world. That is what trust is - that choice to be vulnerable by faith in the testimony of the Word.

Transparency requires vulnerability where we agree with the Comforter to open the doors and allow the healing light of truth to shine into that dark room. Practically speaking, to be transparent before God is to just surrender to what He already knows about us and be confident that His Love remains unwavering -

1 John 3:20 "For if our heart condemn us, God is greater than our heart, and knoweth all things."

Transparency leads to authenticity in our prayer life with God. Our communion with God is a two way communication, whereas shallow religious prayers are just a monologue projected towards God, no different than the pagan prayers of the lost. Authenticity is what we all long for in our spiritual vertical with God because it is the only satisfying element of our lives. Here in this "safe place" we are not afraid of God who deeply sees and knows us thoroughly as He did with Abraham.

Abraham was the friend of God and his relationship was authentic as we see in Genesis 18:17, "And the Lord said, Shall I hide from Abraham that thing which I do?" Abraham was transparent before God resulting in knowing the secrets of God in His plan.

Authenticity costs us our cover - the cover of fig leaves that Adam and Eve used in the Garden of Eden to deal with their guilt and shame. Eventually the fig leaves died and withered away finding themselves naked again. Anything other than honesty and transparency before God is a fig leaf, a substitute for the the true covering of the finished work through Jesus Christ. Surrender your withering fig leaves to the all-seeing compassion of God and you will grow into the next step in your prayer journey.

DAY 13
TOTAL SURRENDER

"Though he slay me, yet will I trust him" - Job 13:15

"O my father, if this cup may not pass away from me, except I drink it, thy will be done." - Matthew 25:42

"All to often secret discontentment can be traced to the the lack of surrender" - Hudson Taylor

"The greatness of the man's power is the measure of his surrender."
— William Booth

There is no negotiating with God. The terms are set - surrender to God's Love, God's Truth, God's Sovereignty. Surrender to that old rugged Cross, rejected and scorned by this world. In our surrender we must surrender our will, emotional feelings, our own religious standards of justice, our limited thought processes, and our perception of who we are.

Anything less is to forfeit the glory of knowing Him and the wisdom that is hid from the wise and the prudent of this world. Surrender as a little child and you will be a partaker of the secrets of the Kingdom of Heaven in prayer.

To surrender absolutely to the King of Kings and the Lord of Lords, is not to be executed by sheer will power nor human determination. It is as it was with Christ, who "through the Eternal Spirit, offered Himself up" - Hebrews 9:14. It is that Spirit that works in us "to will and to do" of His good pleasure.

Surrender is unconditional and without compromise, yet that can only be accomplished by yielding to that Spirit of the Father that led His Son to Calvary - that Spirit of Obedience - 2 Peter 1:2. That Spirit that leads us to surrender is that same "Another" that bore up Peter and carried him where he would not go" - John 21:18.

When that surrender takes place, we hear His voice calling us into prayer, into ministry, and into victory. When we surrender with no excuses, alibis or secret preservations, we discover a deep sense of contentment and peace and all our inner battles end abruptly. For human flesh must yield to the Almighty - Habakkuk 2:20.

Surrender leads to prayer, prayer leads to more surrender.

Surrender ushers in an anointing in your life, a power that cannot be contended with by the devil, the unsurrendered one. All the prayers we could ever pray would not lead us to that answer we seek deep inside. Only surrender to the Omniscient, to the Omnipotent Father who waits to unveil the riches of His salvation and His plan to the surrendered saint can.

There is no more turmoil of battle inside our mortal soul when we bow before the Creator in full submission. O' to the finite man who wars with his secret sins and hidden pride to no avail; the Cross does not empower your flesh to war the good fight of faith. The Cross decimates all your fleshly ability to be godlike. The Cross crushes your enemy and shouts to us "surrender to The Lord Sabaoth and be free!" - John 8.36.

When we bow before Him in prayer, surrender all without reservation, without shame. He then will reveal all, He waits to be gracious...

"All to Jesus I surrender;
All to Him I freely give;
I will ever love and trust Him,
In His presence daily live.
I surrender all,
I surrender all;
All to Thee, my blessed Savior,
I surrender all.
All to Jesus I surrender;
Humbly at His feet I bow,

Worldly pleasures all forsaken;
Take me, Jesus, take me now.
All to Jesus I surrender;
Make me, Savior, wholly Thine;
Let me feel the Holy Spirit,
Truly know that Thou art mine.
All to Jesus I surrender;
Lord, I give myself to Thee;
Fill me with Thy love and power;
Let Thy blessing fall on me.
All to Jesus I surrender;
Now I feel the sacred flame.
Oh, the joy of full salvation!
Glory, glory, to His Name!"

- Judson W. Van DeVenter

DAY 14
STILLNESS & HEARING

"But the Lord is in his holy temple: let all the earth keep silence before him." - Habbakuk 2.20

"There are two kinds of people that keep silence; the one because they have nothing to say, the other because they have too much: the latter is the case in this state; silence is occasioned by excess and not by defect." - Madam Guyon

The inevitable result of true surrender to the loving Hand of God at the Cross, and attentively watching for Him, is stillness. It is then, as we wave our white flag of surrender in the presence of the All Compassionate, our tools of war and defense become quiet and melt away. The sounds of anguish and argument cease and there is a hush on the battlefield of mortal ambition, exertion, attainment, and human achievement. Then only is the sound of His voice heard. This causes us to remember 1 Kings 19:12, that after the earthquake and the fire, there was the still small voice.

This is a significant stillness, not a subdued, defeated, crushed, fearful, or dumb silence. It is a misconception to imagine quietness before God or stillness as a passive state of our soul. Rather it is a stillness that is characterized by the highest and noblest worship of concentration on The Person and the Words of God. Therefore, watchfully hearing Him is the utmost peak of worship in contrast to superfluous speaking or singing as it is portrayed today.

This stark contrast is well illustrated in Luke 10:42, when Martha was cumbered and troubled (Greek, Merimnáō) with attainment for Christ in her home. Mary had chosen the "good part" (Greek, Merís) of listening at His Feet. Thus, our choice this moment is the same: the anxiety of accomplishment for Christ versus obtaining the better portion in quietness as a student before Him in surrender.

Yet, many of us still struggle inwardly, if not also externally, with the lack of stillness of soul. This struggle includes all of our questions, our opinions, our personal sense of justice, and our arguments that we have with God. Due to the stubbornness to bow our knee to the Captain of the Host, we have so much to ask and say to God. But remember, there are no right answers to wrong questions. As a result, the ensuing state of our psyche is a persistent annoying static resonating in our soul that is not properly tuned. This noise is apt to lead to madness if it were not for the worldly distractions that drown out the unsatisfied cries of the soul. Carnal amusement (our English word constructed of two Greek words: A meaning "not" and Muse "to think") becomes our psychological narcotic of choice rather than the stillness and peace of surrender to Him.

The two dominant senses of our mortal construct are seeing and knowing. Both of these senses are addressed by Divine Declaration: "Stand ye still and see -- the Salvation of the Lord" - 2 Chronicles 20:17, and "Be still and know that I am God" - Psalm 46:10. Both of these scriptures satisfy the demands of our senses. Stillness that follows surrender precedes true sight and real knowledge. When we quiet our senses before the Great Communicator we begin to hear the still small voice that Elijah ran for forty days to hear. Stillness of soul is of great importance not because we haven't anything to say to Him, but because we have too much to say to Him.

III. PRAYER ACCESS: ENTERING INTO THE HOLIEST

"Having therefore, brethren, boldness to enter into the holiest by the blood of Jesus, By a new and living way, which he hath consecrated for us, through the veil, that is to say, his flesh; And having an high priest over the house of God; Let us draw near with a true heart in full assurance of faith, having our hearts sprinkled from an evil conscience, and our bodies washed with pure water" - Hebrews 10:19-22

"There must be the inward worship within the shrine if there is to be outward service." - MacLaren

The tabernacle that was built by Moses, under the instruction of God Himself, is a pattern of our access to God for communion with Him at the Holiest of Holies. This tabernacle was the center of the Hebrew camp and traveled with the Jews as they wandered through the desert. This tabernacle was the dwelling of El Shaddai in their midst. The pillar of cloud and the fire by night rising from the tabernacle led them through the treacherous wilderness. It is the pattern, and yet only a shadow, of a better communion for the believer with the Almighty, than in the wilderness for the Hebrews (See: Hebrews 8:1-5; 9:24, 25). Each of the seven articles of furniture in the tabernacle have great meaning. Each one represents Christ and a specific aspect of His ministry that the Jews to this day do not comprehend.

Therefore each item of the tabernacle supports and defines the conditions of invitation for access into His presence in prayer. The three sections of the tabernacle refer to the three ways God meets man. The outer court being where God meets man the sinner, the inner court - the holy place - where God meets man the serving-priest, and finally the inner most - Holiest of Holies, where God meets you and me, the worshipper-priest. As we allow the Spirit to reveal each of the pieces of the sacred furniture we will be ushered into His presence swiftly in prayer.

Namely there are seven items in the tabernacle that we will discuss, one each for the next 7 days. They are listed below in the order of how a priest would enter into the tabernacle:

1) The Altar of Burnt Offering (Exodus 27:1)
2) The Laver (Exodus 30:18)
3) The Table of Showbread (Exodus 25:23)
4) The Lampstand (Exodus 25:31)
5) The Altar of Incense (Exodus 30:1)
6) The Ark of the Covenant (Exodus 25:10)
7) The Mercy Seat (Exodus 25:17

DAY 15
THE ALTAR OF BURNT OFFERING - QUALIFIED
TO DRAW NEAR

"Thou shalt make -- an altar of shittim wood, five cubits long, and five cubits broad; the altar shall be foursquare: and the height thereof shall be three cubits" - Exodus 27:1

When someone approached the tabernacle, they would first notice the linen fabric that surrounded the wall encompassing the outside of the tabernacle. Linen was the material that the priests wore as they ministered. Linen is a fabric that was very comfortable to labor in, it did not cause sweat like the other garments the priests wore. Linen represents for us the grace of the New Covenant with God that nullified the curse of Adam, namely, that he would "work by the sweat of his brow."

The first and foremost truth anyone could see when approaching the tabernacle was that there was "no sweat allowed." The ministry and communion in prayer with God in the Holies was not a result of our hard work, sweat, and duty, It was opened to us by our forerunner, Jesus Christ, who "neither by the blood of goats and calves, but by his own blood he entered in once into the holy place, having obtained eternal redemption for us." - Hebrews 9:12.

The primary truth to understand here is that access is not through any accomplishment or requirement placed on the worshipper. Access is granted freely by One Jesus Christ and His Finished Work. Prayer and communion with God at the mercy seat is founded on the sacrifice, the shedding of the Blood of Jesus Christ and His resurrection.

When the priest entered into the court through the front gate, the altar of the burnt offering was the dominant item of the outer court. It was the center of attention, unavoidable. It was the emphasis that stated: to go further, there must be absolute surrender, death, sacrifice, the spilling of blood, and

the complete burning of the sacrifice. The outer court was filled with
the fragrance of the burning of the offerings of many bulls and goats. The altar itself was very simple in its design. It was a box made of acacia wood overlaid with bronze, 7.5 feet square, standing 4.5 feet high, and had four horns pointing outward at each corner. Acacia (sometimes referred to as "shittim wood") is a hard, incorruptible, indestructible wood that grows in the Sinai Desert. It beautifully points to the vulnerability and trust of the Hebrews towards their God as they moved through the Sinai. This wood was used by Noah through Divine instruction to build the ark that saved him, his family, and the animals on board from the perils of the flood.

Hence, wood symbolizes humanity. It beautifully portrays the humanity of Christ, who came from "a root out of dry ground" - Isaiah 53:2, and was sinless in His human nature - Hebrews 4:15, 7:26. The indestructibility of the wood speaks of Christ in His humanity, who withstood the sacrifice on the cross, offered Himself wholly (John 10:18) passed through the decay of the grave (Acts 2:31) and was victoriously raised (Romans 4:25) for our justification.

The altar was covered with bronze which represents the Word of Judgment . This portrays the finality of the sacrifice which was satisfactory before God. On the altar itself were the four horns that pinned the sacrifice to the place of offering. This concurs with the truth that our sacrifice, Jesus the Man, was nailed to the cross voluntarily for the joy that was set before Him. It is powerful to note that the horns that tied the offering down pointed outward, having a signature that shows the reaching out of the message of the altar to the four corners of the world - the Gospel of Grace in world missions.

As worshippers in prayer and intercession with Him, we must clearly understand that the all-encompassing truth of our worship is that we share the "sweat-less" yoke that Christ bore. The environment in the tabernacle was not an environment of sweat and laborious duty. It had a flow. Such is prayer. It is a flow and is as lightweight as linen. Linen can easily be stained and so is our ministry in the tabernacle as a worshipper-priest. Any fleshly ambition or self-occupation will spot our garment and disqualify us in the flow of ministry in prayer. There is a condition here we see in the outer court, it is the sacrifice of the Lamb of God, once and for all. It was effective in every way and left nothing unfinished. If we do not understand the altar of the burnt offering we will live bound to our plaguing former sins, our present struggles, and we will not be able to proceed into effective prayer. We will be halted at the outer court. The sad truth is that it is precisely where many Christians today dwell because they do not understand the sacrifice made for them to enter into worship.

Therefore we draw near to Him with our guilty consciousness, cleansed and purged by the sprinkling of the blood from that altar of the burnt offering, the Cross. We draw near in prayer to God because we leave all our baggage at the altar; we have been made pure with no more consciousness of sin - Hebrews 10:2. Praise God!

DAY 16
THE LAVER - CLEANSING AND MIND RENEWAL

Thou shalt also make a laver of brass, and his foot also of brass, to wash withal: and thou shalt put -- it between the tabernacle of the congregation and -- the altar, and thou shalt put water therein. - Exodus 30:18

After we have understood surrender at the all consuming fiery altar, and the forgiveness and clearing of sins, we may move on to the next article in the outer courtyard. Standing before the worshipper, between the altar and the door to the inner court stands a simple wash basin. This laver was described briefly in the account of Exodus. No measurements were given, except that it was to be made of bronze and have a footing of bronze. The purpose of the laver was to hold water for washing. The priests were to wash their hands and feet in the outer court before they were able to enter into the inner court to minister - Exodus 30:19, 20. This laver was originally fashioned from the mirrors of the women who served at the doorway of the tent of meeting - Exodus 38:8. This is significant because the laver was not only a place of washing, but also a place of reflection into the mirror of the Word of God. Here is the true reflection of who the worshipper-priest really is, an able minister, meet for the Master's use.

The cleansing at the laver was different than the cleansing at the altar. The altar was for sin, whereas the laver was for the washing of the hands and feet that became dirty periodically from everyday defilement from the dusty world system. This was the meaning of John 13, when Jesus washed his disciples feet and not their whole body, as Peter so eagerly desired. When Paul wrote to the Ephesians, "That he might sanctify and cleanse it with the washing of water by the word" - Ephesians 5:26, he was referring to this very item, the laver.

See, we are purged from our sins once and for all by the sacrifice at the altar, but we need a continual daily,

hourly, cleansing that comes only though the Word that
He has spoken to us - John 15:3. If we do not allow this cleansing by the Word spoken, then we have no part in Him in the inner court of prayer - John 13:8.

This brings us to an important point. Often, as worshippers, we appreciate and understand the finality of the offering for sins on the cross. We proclaim it and it is central to our Christianity, yet we fail to understand the importance of the cleansing that must take place inside our soul from the effects and damages of sin. Before we enter into the inner court in prayer and abide there, there must be a deep, continuing catharsis in our soul - a cleansing that comes through the spoken Word. When we allow the Rhema of the spoken word to penetrate us in a personal way, we are, cleansed and healed from the sins we were forgiven of. If not, we experience spiritual death, although we are, in fact, forgiven - Exodus 30:20.

Just as we are to surrender daily to the altar in the outer court, we are to surrender daily to the spoken Word, which is the water that cleanses us continually from the filth in the world that we come into contact with daily. The cleansing that comes from the water of the Word sanctifies us and prepares us for the inner court. This renews the spirit of our mind - Ephesians 4:23.

Unfortunately, many believers never really enter into the inner court to worship. Experientially, they fail to or enter into intimacy with God at the mercy seat because they are occupied in the outer court with themselves and their poor reflections, uninformed of their forgiveness at the altar.

Surrender is the key word for both the altar and the laver. Without first surrendering at these two places, and without having spiritual truths revealed to us by His Spirit, we cannot enter into the inner court of mind renewal, prayer, worship, and communion. We will only be standing on the outside in self-consciousness, not God-consciousness.

DAY 17
THE LAMPSTAND - THE LIFE-LIGHT OF MEN

"And thou shalt make a candlestick of pure gold: of beaten work shall the candlestick be made: his shaft, and his branches, his bowls, his knops, and his flowers, shall be of the same". - Exodus 25:31

We, as worshipper-priests enter into the inner court, the Holy Place, having a renewed mind and having experienced a cleansing externally as well as internally. No one but the priest was allowed into the Holy Place. So we in like fashion, have left behind morbid self-consciousness that was burdensome in its self-occupation, and we have entered into the enclosed inner court. Here we discover three articles: the lampstand to the left, the table of shewbread to the right, and in the center, before the veil, is the altar of incense. These three articles are full of meaning and importance for us in their function, as well their symbolism, as we draw near with a heart fully assured.

The key description we observe in the Holy Place is "continual." Each article had to be tended to and cared for, not left neglected. The lampstand needed to be continually lit and trimmed. The table of shewbread needed to be continually supplied, and the altar of incense needed to be continually burning fragrance. These characteristics of the ministry of the worshipper-priest emphasize our abiding and tarrying in the Holy Place. Here, in prayer, we are set apart from the world and its constant attention on the flesh and its fallen deeds in the outer court of self-occupation.

When entering the Holy Place of the inner court, we first notice the bright candlestick, the lampstand that lights the table of shewbread and the altar of incense. The lampstand provided light for the priest to move about and minister at each article of furniture found in the Holy Pace. The instruction for the lampstand was that it be beaten and shaped from one piece of gold that was about 75 lbs. in weight. There were six shafts that branched outward and upward from one main shaft, that was straight and most likely the tallest, of the other six. The crafting of this article required the utmost skill because if just one shaft was ill-made, it would hinder the flow of oil to the candle. The lampstand was to be tended to in the mornings and evenings so that the ashes could be removed, the wicks trimmed and the oil be replenished, that the "light would ever be burning" - Leviticus 6:13.

Due to the enclosed nature of the inner court, it was dark and there was not much, if any, natural light from outside. The lampstand was to be the sole light in the Holy Place. No outer light would do, it was forbidden. Isaiah 50:11 points to this when he writes of the woes of walking in the light of a self-made fire. Light in the Holy Place could not be counterfeited.

This lampstand is so filled with meaning and symbolism we do not have time or space to write about it here, but suffice it to say, that the candlestick represents the Life-Light of Jesus Christ. Most of the other articles in the tabernacle were made with acacia wood, but the lampstand was made of one piece of pure beaten gold. This, without question, speaks of the Divinity of Christ revealed by the Spirit, beaten and formed from one source, pure in nature, hidden from the eyes of the outer court. The oil symbolizing the flow of the Holy Spirit, was to be continually flowing through carefully crafted shafts to feed the ever burning flame. The seven candles represent the complete Finished Work of Jesus Christ for His people, thus this truth was to illuminate the entire Holy Place continually via the flow of the oil of the Holy Spirit.

The reality of the Life of Christ being the "Light of Men" - John 1:4, is the only permitable source of illumination in the Holy Place. Other light would be rejected and would be a false light, like Satan, who masquerades as the angel of light - 2 Corinthians 11.14, yet in truth, he is a counterfeit.

As we enter the Holy Place of the inner court, our ministry of prayer and communion with God begins in intimacy, enlightened by the leading of the Holy Spirit's light, to the sacred articles in the Holy Place. This means our communion with God is a finished work communion, illuminated by the Eternal Light of Christ Himself.   We may bask in His presence and freely enjoy our abiding ministry of prayer in the inner court!

DAY 18
TABLE OF SHOWBREAD - COMMUNION

"Thou shalt also make a table of shittim wood: two cubits shall be the length thereof, and a cubit the breadth thereof, and a cubit and a half the height thereof". - Exodus 25:23

The table of shewbread is a striking picture of New Testament truth for the worshipper-priest. The light from the lampstand lights up the table of shewbread that is situated directly across from the lampstand on the north side. It is as if the lampstand is accentuating the table of communion. The table was constructed from the hard, close-grained acacia wood used for many other articles in the tabernacle. The wood was then covered with pure gold. The table itself was three feet long, 1.5 feet in breadth, and 2 feet, 3 inches high so that when the priest was ministering at this table it was low enough that it required a measure of bowing down and over to properly reach the shewbread.

On the table itself was bread. "And thou shalt take fine flour, and bake twelve cakes thereof: two tenth deals shall be in one cake. And thou shalt set them in two rows, six on a row, upon the pure table before the Lord." - Leviticus 24:5,6. Each loaf or cake had about four quarts of fine flour in it. This flour was beaten rigorously to fine powder, signifying the extreme suffering of Jesus our Messiah, no lumps or impurities in the flour at all. Every Sabbath day, hot, fresh loaves were placed on the table, in two rows of six each, and the past week's bread was to be eaten by the priests in that place set aside as holy. This scene undeniably reminds us of the Last Supper with Jesus as He, our High Priest, ate in a place set aside as holy, in communion with His disciples. The twelve loaves of shewbread were representative of each of the tribes of Israel. We can see the precious picture of God's great desire for intimate communion with His people and the New Testament worshipper-priest.

At certain Levitical ceremonies, on the new moons, and the morning and evening offerings, a pressed grape
drink was poured out in the Holy Place, on the floor of the tabernacle, by the table of shewbread. Just as this drink was being poured out in the Holy Place, the lamb was sacrificed and being burned on the altar of burnt offering. How much clearer can the picture be of the Lamb of God being slain for us and His Precious Redeeming Blood being poured out?

While the priest served in the Holy Place of the inner court at the table of shewbread, he did so in the light provided by the lampstand. We, also, as worshipper-priests, enjoy our communion in prayer with Christ, our High Priest, provided by God Himself, in the light of the work that was completed at the Cross, our altar - 1 John 1:7.

Communion, the partaking of the bread, which is Christ Himself, is a critical part of our tarrying in the Holy Place. It is the inner court life of prayer and meditation that bids us by the Divine Light to come and dine with the God of Israel Himself at His table of grace.

DAY 19
THE ALTAR OF INCENSE - THE FRAGRANCE
OF PRAYER

And thou shalt make an altar to burn incense upon: of shittim wood shalt thou make -- it. - Exodus 30:1

The golden altar or the altar of incense was the last article in the order of the Holy Place before entering in through the veil that separated the Holy Place from the Holiest of Holies. The altar was directly in line with the mercy seat that was situated in the innermost sanctum.

This altar of incense was made of the same shittim wood or acacia wood as other articles in the tabernacle and covered in fine gold. Again we see the great care and meaning in the construction of each item in the Holy Place. The rings and the staves gave the altar a characteristic of mobility. There is an obvious connection between this altar and the altar of the burnt offering in the outer court. Both were places of sacrifice with four horns, the difference being that the altar in the outer court was for sin and the altar in the Holy Place was for prayer and worship. The altar of incense was much smaller in size than the altar of burnt offering in the outer court. It was only eighteen inches square and three feet high, but nine inches larger than the Ark of the Covenant and the table of shewbread.

The incense that was to be continually offered on this altar was made of stacte, onycha, galbanum, and frankincense, seasoned with salt. Each spice has great meaning which we cannot address here, but perhaps later. This composition was sacred and was forbidden to be substituted for any other fragrance. It was sweet in smell, pure in substance, and holy by nature. No one in the camp was to replicate this incense or offer any other type of incense on this altar, lest they suffer the consequence of being cut off from Israel.

The meaning of this golden altar of incense has much to teach the worshipper-priest. Being the fifth item in the tabernacle, we immediately see the significance of the altar as being an altar of grace. Grace must always be understood as the platform for prayer and worship. Therefore at this altar of worship and prayer, there is no more awareness of sin and shame - Hebrews 10:2!

Sweet, pure, and sacred prayer always precedes entry into His presence. It is the last and nearest place to the mercy seat. This is the place of merciful intercession that we see symbolized by the high priest for Israel. This altar having four horns, as well as the altar in the outer court, points to world missions. World evangelism and the Gospel reaching every nation was always a part of the high priest's ministry of prayer! Prayer is not just for ourselves and those in the camp, but also for those lost in this world that need the Gospel of Grace.

Prayer and worship certainly usher us into the presence of the Most Holy. It is the culmination of the first four objects in the tabernacle. Without understanding clearly, by the illumination of the Holy Spirit, each articles' function and meaning, we cannot enter into the full depth of prayer God has intended.

Prayer supersedes the self-consciousness of sin and unworthiness in the outer court and takes precedence over the labor of service in the inner court. The outer court relates to all that is world-conscious: the physical, the imperfect, and the limitations of our body of sin that has been crucified at the Cross. In the inner court, there is the labor of the soul-life, where there may be an over-abundance of self-awareness as we serve. So many Christians can be overtaken with serving in the inner court, but never advancing into the fellowship at the mercy seat.

It is prayer that delivers us from self-awareness and speedily brings us before the throne of grace, the mercy seat. It is prayer and worship at the altar of incense that takes us from the inner court of our ministry and leads us to stand before Him, the object of our ultimate adoration, the One whom we desire.

DAY 20
THE ARK OF THE COVENANT - A
FINISHED WORK

And they shall make an ark of shittim wood: two cubits and a half shall be the length thereof, and a cubit and a half the breadth thereof, and a cubit and a half the height thereof. And thou shalt overlay -- it with pure gold, within and without shalt thou overlay it, and shalt make upon it a crown of gold round about. - Exodus 25:10

The Ark of the Covenant was the sixth item in the tabernacle. We will afford ourselves a bit more time in this chapter to properly deal with this most holy of all the furniture. It was made of thorny, rough, and durable acacia wood overlaid with pure gold. The ark had rings on the sides for the poles to carry when the children of Israel were on the move in the wilderness. Serving as a lid on the top of the Ark of the Covenant was the solid gold mercy seat, which we will elaborate on in the next chapter. The ark resided in the Holiest of Holies, a room 15 square feet, without light due to the opaque veil that excluded all, even the light from outside the tabernacle. The inner sanctum remained dark unless the light of the Shekinah Glory of His presence filled it - Exodus 40:34,35; Psalm 18:11.

On the Day of Atonement, once a year, when the priest would enter from the Holy Place to the Holiest Place of the Ark of the Covenant, he carried a censer, an incense burner (some scholars differ on the exact procedure here). As he passed through the veil, the incense burner would precede the priest into the Holiest Place. This clearly represents the path of fragranced prayer. When the high priest entered, he had to peel back the veil to permit the light from the lampstand to flood into the dark chamber.

Yet from the moment that the veil was rent from top to bottom upon Christ's death in Matthew 27;51, the Holiest of Holies was lightened forever by that eternal lampstand, Jesus Christ. The life of Jesus, our forerunner, is the Light that lights up our path of prayer as a worshipper-priest to the Ark of the Covenant itself, the secret place of His presence - Psalm 91.

The ark was of special importance because sealed underneath the lid of the mercy seat, were three very significant items. We must properly understand the meaning of these items historically and why they are sealed underneath the mercy seat, lest we miss the mark in prayer.

The three items were:

1. The two tables of stone, the Testimony, namely the Ten Commandments (Exodus 25:16; Deuteronomy 31:26)
2. The memorial jar of manna (Exodus 16:33)
3. Aaron's rod that budded (Numbers 17)

Please note here that these items were sealed inside the ark and no one was allowed to look inside for the consequence was instantaneous death. These items were sealed inside on purpose to represent to the worshipper-priest that in each of these memorials was a completed, finished work of God, commanded to be eternally sealed in their accomplished state. We can see each of the items having been fulfilled in Jesus Christ Himself.

Let's look at these items briefly:

The tablets of stone - The Testimony: This was the Law that Christ had fulfilled in Himself - Romans 8:3; 10:4. Thus it is sealed, finished.

The memorial jar of manna: This is the picture of Jesus, the Bread that came from Heaven - John 6:31-33, that dwelt among us and was broken for us. As the manna is sealed, so we no longer know Jesus after the flesh - 2 Corinthians 5:16. We walk by faith in daily rhema-manna.

Aaron's rod that budded: The priest Aaron, who represented the priesthood of the coming High Priest, was validated through his rod of authority in that it budded and bloomed in the very presence of God. The rod budded in the tabernacle of the congregation, or the term used in Numbers 17:8, the tabernacle of witness. This undoubtedly testifies of the power of Jesus Christ in the tabernacle of witness in that He passed through death and rose again bearing first-fruits. This is the power of resurrection life that operates in the priesthood God has chosen - Hebrews 7:16. It too is sealed inside the Ark, "once and for all", never to be debated again. Hallelujah!

Therefore we may boldly say Jesus is our ark, the Ark of the Covenant with our God! - Hebrews 9:4

The Ark of the Covenant was the center of all that Israel did, and wherever Israel went. It was the symbol of God's central presence, power, and communion with His people - Exodus 25:22. There the Lord rejoiced in the midst of His people with singing - Zephaniah 3:17. When Israel set forward into march, the tribes moved out in a specific order and rank, completely surrounding the Levites who were carrying the tabernacle. God Himself literally tabernacled among His people.

For example, as the Hebrews approached the great Jordan river, the Ark was to be brought a sizable distance away from the people, although within eyesight. It was the blessing and authority for Israel and their advantage in warfare. All the inhabitants of the land that were soon to become the Hebrews' were in fear of their God. The Ark was to be carried on the shoulders of the priests. This is a beautiful picture that God mandated that He dwell upon our shoulders as He did with Christ - Isaiah 9:7 and that it not be driven or pulled by an animal or mechanized cart. As believer-priests God desires to dwell upon us, rest upon us as a dove quietly lights upon its perch.

Thus it is clear to us that the Ark of the Covenant was a type of Jesus Christ Himself - who tabernacled among us - John 1:14,16. God rejoices among His People through His Son Jesus and He is mighty in our midst. He is the center of all we do and where we go. Jesus is the sign of God's delight and His power among us. Within Himself, this Wonderful Savior, the work has been completely perfected and we may approach boldly to the mercy seat of grace.   Praise God!

"It is indeed infinite mercy that God is come so near you as to dwell in your flesh" - John Flavel

DAY 21
THE MERCY SEAT - THE MEETING PLACE
OF HIS PRESENCE

And there I will meet with thee, and I will commune with thee from above the mercy seat, from between the two cherubims which are upon the ark of the testimony - Exodus 25.22

There are a myriad of places where people want to meet God in prayer; the place of their service, their ministry, their emotions, their religious and spiritual experiences, their good endeavors, their humanitarian deeds, even their well-meaning intentions. But there is only one place that El Shaddai has conditioned to be the place where infinite love and grace will meet with sinners, the mercy seat - Leviticus 16:2 and Exodus 25:21,22.

The mercy seat in the Hebrew context meant "a covering" and that was exactly what it did. The seat was pure, solid gold differing from the Ark of the Covenant in that the seat had no wood in its constitution. This is significant because the place that God met man was a place that frail man had nothing to do with achieving (wood) but only God Himself was able to bring this to pass in all of His Divinity (gold).

The seat was exactly the size of the Ark beneath it. It covered the Ark and it's contents perfectly in its length and in its width. This is what mercy does, it always covers and seals the judgement that inevitably comes without the presence of mercy. Without the mercy seat, there was death - 1 Samuel 6:19.

Now when the worshipper-priest enters the Holiest of Holies he sees a sealed article, an Ark that was covered. He saw a finished and perfected work that hid those things of an old covenant. Those things were not only covered from the sight of man, but also from the sight of God.

On top of the Ark and the slab of pure gold was the seat that became the throne of God where the

Shekinah Glory of God descended. It was there where two cherubim stood, made of beaten and hammered gold, with wings spread covering the mercy seat. There, between their wings, was where the blood was sprinkled seven times, once a year on the Day of Atonement, the very spot that the cherubim fixed their gaze upon. This mercy seat is the focus of Heaven and of all His angels. Mercy is the only thing that God sees when He meets man.

This throne is the center of the tabernacle. It is the focal point, the place where we the worshipper-priests go to worship and to minister in the Holiest of Holies. This is the goal, this is the place that God said He would meet us. God categorically will not meet man anywhere else outside of His mercy and His grace. This is where we meet Him in prayer. Nowhere else will God agree to meet us, but right there at the throne of mercy. This where we meet Him in the time of need - Hebrews 4:16. This is the throne of grace, where prayers are heard and answered. This is the place of refuge that we flee to when we are pursued by the enemy of our souls.

The whole journey into His holy presence is culminated here - at the mercy seat, where our sins are blotted out by the Blood that was applied there, where the Law that was written against us is covered, and the manna that was hidden from us is now made manifest and the Levitical priesthood of service ends. It all ends here, at the mercy seat! All our fellowship and communion with God begins here, here at the throne of grace.

IV. WAGING WAR IN PRAYER

"Let us, therefore, forsake the vanity of the crowd and their false teachings and turn back to the word delivered to us from the beginning, 'watching unto prayer' and continuing steadfast in fasting, beseeching fervently the all-seeing God 'to lead us not into temptation', even as the Lord said, 'The spirit indeed is willing, but the flesh is weak.'" —Polycarp (69-156).

I may no longer depend on pleasant impulses to bring me before the Lord. I must rather respond to principles I know to be right, whether I feel them to be enjoyable or not. – Jim Elliot

DAY 22
WATCHING WITH HIM IN PRAYER

"And he cometh unto the disciples, and findeth them asleep, and saith unto peter, what, could ye not watch with me one hour? Watch and pray, that ye enter not into temptation:the spirit indeed is willing, but the flesh is weak" - Matthew 26.41

"Prayer without watching is hypocrisy, and watching without prayer is presumption." - William Jay

The arrival into His presence at the sweet mercy seat is only one aspect of our prayer journey. It is there where it really begins for the worshipper. There the worshipper becomes a warrior in spiritual warfare. It is there in prayer we learn that the weapons of our warfare are not carnally commanded. It is prayer that we see in the list of Paul's armor in Ephesians 6, that is the secret weapon. When we begin to pray we face the onslaught of Satanic forces because Satan believes in the power of prayer more than any of us ever will.

Those that learn watching in prayer enter into another phase of prayer. They move from worshipper to warrior. Those that learn this secret of watching are most threatening to the forces of the accuser. You will note that the primary tactic that our adversary, the devil, uses to thwart watching-prayer is sleepiness, dullness, and lethargy. This is largely due to the fact that the novice in prayer is always looking by sight and waiting for the answers that are self-pleasing and preference-oriented. They miss the action because they are looking in the wrong direction and the enemy slips in unnoticed.

To draw a little perspective to the immense importance of watching in prayer, Jesus, in Matthew 26, in His hour of conflict in prayer, goes three times to His disciples and petitions them to watch in prayer. The battle for the cross was won not at Calvary but in the Garden of Gethsemane. Jesus was inundated with a flood of demonic hosts trying to steer him off the course to the cross. This is when He asked His disciples to pray. There is something that we see here. Jesus in prayer and in battle wanted His disciples engaged in prayer and discernment because of the host of demons pitted against Him in the garden to try to kill Him.

When we learn watching-prayer, we learn to pray with Jesus in his hour of personal heaviness. Imagine that there are times today when Jesus is burdened for people faltering in their lives, cities and nations where there is no witness for the Gospel, and situations where none stand for the truth. He is our Great Intercessor and when He is moved with compassion or He is grieved, he goes to His watchers, his disciples, and calls on them to "watch and pray" with Him. There are not many that have this great privilege, that are asked to pray in this hour with Jesus, but his three intimate disciples were: Peter, James, and John. Watchers in prayer are those few that are God's "special forces" in warfare, they don't sleep when the rest of the army slumbers in their barracks. That is actually the connotation of the word "watch" in the original script of Matthew 26:38 - grēgoreúō. This word means to be set on the special towers of the walls, on sober lookout for enemy movements and ambushes. These watchers stood on guard to the point of sleep deprivation. O! Can we hear our Saviour say "watch and pray"? Can we hear Him softly tread to our place of slumber and with a touch of His hand in the late night hour say, "watch with me"? Oh Spirit of watching make us to hear His voice a short distance away pleading with His Father in that Garden. Stir us to watch with Him!

"I come to the garden alone
While the dew is still on the roses
And the voice I hear falling on my ear
The Son of God discloses...
I'd stay in the garden with Him

Though the night around me be falling,
But He bids me go; through the voice of woe
His voice to me is calling." - C. Austin Miles

My wife and I were recently in Puerto Rico and one of the most impressive sights for me was the fortress at San Juan. It guarded the gateway to the Caribbean. From the watch towers at the peak of the fort, hundreds and hundreds of miles could be monitored along a 180 degree span of the sea's horizon in search for enemy vessels' movements. This is what is explicitly meant by Jeremiah 51:12 - "Set up the standard upon the walls of Babylon, make the watch strong, set up the watchmen, prepare the ambushes: for the Lord hath both devised and done -- that which he spoke against the inhabitants of Babylon." Jesus also referred to this in the context of what he said to his three: "watch and pray that you enter not into temptation." When we exercise ourselves in watchful prayer we effectively avoid and escape so much unnecessary temptation.

Ezra, the author of Psalm 119 and the leader of the Jews returning to Jerusalem to rebuild, was also a watcher in prayer when he said that his eyes "prevent the night watches" - Psalm 119:148.

In the case of Gideon, God could not use any of his army except those that looked to the horizon in careful watch as they drank the water from their hands at the brook - Judges 7:6

Therefore, there are those few as we read about in Proverbs 8:34, that are the blessed watchers that receive a measure of wisdom and skill in warfare -

"Blessed is the man that heareth me, watching daily at my gates, waiting at the posts of my doors."

Watching in prayer means we leave the realm of the feeling, the sullenness of passive human nature and we stir ourselves up in attentive watching for the next Word from Christ our Commander and the movement of the foe. The watcher is one who has much insight, compassion, loyalty, and wisdom. He may not speak much or express much of his opinion, but he watches and prays with His Master in the most critical hour. The watcher is a true friend indeed, often an unseen aid in the spectrum of warfare against the Savior and His Church in this world.

DAY 23
THE IMPACT OF PRAYER

"The effectual fervent prayer of a righteous man availeth much." - James 5:16b

"It is possible to move men, through God, by prayer alone." - J. Hudson Taylor

Christians today wholly underestimate the power and impact they could have on the two invisible kingdoms. Perhaps it is because of their incessant orientation to the visible and comprehensible realm of living. No doubt, the kingdom of darkness endeavors to shroud the effectiveness of just one prayer, even by the weakest saint. If the saint only understood the damage it could do to that kingdom, and the victory it could have, with one heart-felt prayer toward the throne of mercy, he would truly pray without ceasing.

Volumes of books could be written on the topic of prayer's power. Countless stories could be told of answers to prayers: healings, salvations, deliverances, and provisions that have come from the prayers of God's People. The God that dwells between the cherubim waits to be gracious and eagerly desires to impact the world today, yet He has in some respects limited Himself to the simple prayers of frail men and women.

The simple act of prayer is the greatest act that the Church could do today to impact this fleeting world. This is why we have found ourselves here before a throne of grace. It is the Spirit of Intercession that has brought us to this place of the Holiest of Holies. It was not ourselves that began this journey in prayer, but God's passionate Spirit that prays with groanings that cannot be worded. He has drawn us here to prayer. We thought it was our own selfish need and troubles, but it was the wooing of the Spirit of His Son that has been our unction to press into His inner court, only to discover that it was His Spirit that caused us to do His bidding.

The secret to moving people is not to wrangle with them about God, but to first converse alone with God about them. This is the power of evangelism. Evangelism and missions preceded by prayer is by far the most effective ministry. Prayer and missions are the inseparable married pair; if there is to be spiritual fruit, they must never be divorced from each other. To move a city, a nation, a family, or a soul, we first and foremost must move God in prayer. In turn, God moves the heart of the man. For is it not that the heart of the most powerful king lays in the hand of God and that He turns it however He pleases? - Proverbs 21:1

This begs the question of free will and God's will. It understandably could be asked as we pray, "is this God's will?" This is the impenetrable gate that so easily thwarts the timid and rational, yet it is the very reason we must cast ourselves upon the altar of mercy and petition Him. For it is when we do so, we hear from God, the God who loves this world, souls abundantly more than we could ever love. There at the feet of the Most Holy, we uncover the hidden Will of God and only then can we pray to that end.

Here is a curious example of what is being said - Exodus 32:9-10. "And the Lord said unto Moses, I have seen -- this people, and, behold, it is a stiff-necked people: Now therefore let me alone, that my wrath may wax hot against them, and that I may consume them: and I will make -- of thee a great nation." God is moved against the Hebrew nation to destroy it in His anger. Yet Moses went before God and petitioned the God of Israel - "And Moses besought -- -- the Lord his God, and said, Lord, why doth thy wrath wax hot against thy people, which thou hast brought forth out of the land of Egypt

with great power, and with a mighty hand? Wherefore should the Egyptians speak,
and say, For mischief did he bring them out, to slay -- them in the mountains, and to consume them from the face of the earth? Turn from thy fierce wrath, and repent of this evil against thy people. Remember Abraham, Isaac, and Israel, thy servants, to whom thou sworest by thine own self, and saidst unto them, I will multiply -- your seed as the stars of heaven, and all this land that I have spoken of will I give unto your seed, and they shall inherit it forever." - Exodus 32:11-14. Moses, in rehearsing before God His own Covenant with His People, moved God to change His Mind. Moses moved a nation by moving his Lord. Then again, in Numbers 16:41-45, because Moses knew how to speak to the Lord as a man speaks with his friend - Exodus 33:11.

God seeks "to and fro throughout the earth" for an intercessor, that He would not destroy the land - to make up the gaping gulf - to make up the gap in prayer - Ezekiel 22:20. He is looking today for prayer intercessors, intimate conversants, yes, He is doing more than looking; He is drawing them into His inner throne room to share with them a secret of His love for this lost world that is bounding towards the gates of Hell.

For when He has drawn us to Himself, He purges us, cleanses us and tells us His burden for people. It is then that His "will is done on Earth as it is in Heaven."

"Prayer lays hold of God's plan and becomes the link between His will and its accomplishment on earth. Amazing things happen, and we are given the privilege of being the channels of the Holy Spirit's prayer." ~ Elisabeth Elliot

DAY 24
THE RESISTANCE TO PRAYER

"Likewise, ye husbands, dwell with them according to knowledge, giving honor unto the wife, as unto the weaker vessel, and as being heirs together of the grace of life; that your prayers be not hindered." - 1 Peter 3:7

"Without a counselor to tell us what was wrong, God Himself began to heal our marriage. And with every prayer we prayed together, Jesus became that third strand of a braided cord, binding us tightly together and giving us strength. With this increased spiritual bonding came emotional intimacy. The heart-to-heart connection with my husband that I had desired for so long slowly began to become a reality." - Cheri Fuller

Knowing the impact of prayer and it's devastating effect on the kingdom of darkness, it is of no wonder that prayer is to be so hindered and resisted by the prince of the power of the air. Of all the efforts of the church of Christ, none are of greatest effect than the bending of the knee in communion and intercession. It is to be the primary labor of the church.

Yet, how would the prayers of the saints be hindered? In what way? How could it be that the most powerful weapon of the church could be thwarted by our foe?

First it is to be hindered by none other than in the sphere of marriage. It is no mistake that the Apostle Peter in 1 Peter 3:7 writes that husbands ought to "live considerately with [your wives], with an intelligent recognition [of the marriage relation], honoring the woman as [physically] the weaker, but [realizing that you] are joint heirs of the grace (God's unmerited favor) of life" (Amplified). Many prayers of families and married couples are stonewalled due to the simple fact of the deficiency of humility, love, and honor in marriage.

More than once have hyper-spiritual concepts and the lack of forgiveness in marriage hindered prayers. A wife that complains that her husband is not spiritual or that he doesn't take godly headship and compares him to other men in the church is only hurting herself. She should acknowledge the fact that her spirituality is not recognized by God. Her only prayer should be "Lord forgive my self-righteousness."

On the other hand, a leader in the assembly that considers his wife an extra weight keeping him from

serving God in the ministry is in error. Until his attitude
changes to "loving consideration" and "intelligent recognition" of his "heir of grace," his ministry will not be endued with the blessing of God's anointing and his prayers as well will be hindered.

As God would have it, in His Wisdom, He has created marriage to be the theater of where His heart and Word be manifested. Humility in relationship is the traction of our prayer life and
spirituality; there the "rubber meets the road." Only Heaven itself will unveil the impact of the petitions and intercessions of a praying family.

Someone once described the process of a couple praying together as "two people suddenly becoming naked spiritually with each other as they bare their soul before God in their presence." There is much hinderance to couples praying together today. Richard Foster put it well: "We today yearn for prayer and hide from prayer. We are attracted to it and repelled by it. We believe prayer is something we should do, even something we want to do, but it seems like a chasm stands between us and actually praying." Prayer together takes humility and transparency.

It would be of much ease for our flesh to pray with great labor yet despise our mate. In this case our prayers are hindered by the Accuser of the Brethren and our petitions go no further than the sound of our voices.

Why is this? Because God resists the proud. Pride is the monster sin that God hates. "But he giveth more grace. Wherefore he saith, God resisteth the proud,

112

but giveth grace unto the humble" - James 4:6. Often people blame the devil and his demons for the resistance they experience when in reality it is the Almighty Himself
that stands against the believer due to his arrogant attitude.

Prayer that is effective and powerful is prayer that comes from the heart and lips of the broken sinner saved by grace. "And the publican, standing afar off, would not lift up so much as his eyes unto heaven, but smote upon his breast, saying, God be merciful to me a sinner." - Luke 18:13

Satan trembles the most when he sees the weakest sinner on his knees praying. For God looks to the broken in spirit and humble of heart. Thus, even before we take into account any pervading sin in a person's life or their beseting habits; pride is the culprit that causes the prayers of the saint to stumble. When we detect our prayers are being unanswered, we ought to examine within the sphere of the Finished Work of Christ to determine whether there is the subtle spectre of pride that has gone unconfessed within our heart. Humility and brokenness with a contrite spirit are the keys that open any locked door of prayer. It melts the iron-clad heavens revealing a throne of grace ready and waiting to be gracious to the lowliest of soul.

"Nothing tends more to cement the hearts of Christians than praying together. Never do they love one another so well as when they witness the outpouring of each other's hearts in prayer." - Charles Finney

DAY 25
GREATLY BELOVED IN PRAYER

"At the beginning of your prayers, the word [giving an answer] went forth, and I have come to tell you, for you are greatly beloved. Therefore consider the matter and understand the vision." - Daniel 9:23 (Amplified)

"Prayer is nothing more than turning our heart toward God and receiving in turn His love" - Madam Guyon

It is of primary importance that we see that before any warfare be waged in the matter of Daniel and the vision, the angel speaks to Daniel stating that he is greatly loved and that the "command" went out at the beginning of his prayer. These two points are foundational in the understanding of warfare in prayer. Otherwise, we find ourselves in a struggle that we have no understanding of nor the matter of the vision to follow.

It has been said that in the time of war there is no love. It is quite sufficient to state it is every man for himself in survival in many respects. It is kill or be killed in combat and the outcome is only one of two: live or die.

Yet in prayer it is of another kind and the method is completely different. The foundation of warfare in prayer is not one of cut-throat survival, but a foundation of love. Before the vision was to be communicated and understood, the Lord wanted Daniel to know that he was "greatly loved."

No vision or battle in our lives can ever be effective and victorious if we do not first have the pervasive understanding that we as God's men and women are "greatly loved." That "great love" of God creates a secure sphere about us that becomes a faithful foothold when the winds and woes of the battle swarm about us.

The Apostle Paul writes in Ephesians 3.17 "that being rooted and grounded in Christ's Love" is the beginning of all comprehension in verse 18. There is no greater foundation in a fluid environment such as war than the love of God. From the perspective of God's Love, we are perceiving with discernment and proper understanding the vision and the warfare that ensues.

The strategy of the Enemy in warfare is to divide and conquer.
That is always the method of the Enemy who is outnumbered. He wages guerrilla warfare, in the air via projections, so that we are alienated from the life of God in our minds, thus succumbing to the vanity of thinking that God is not for us - Ephesians 4:18. When God's child no longer believes in the all-encompassing love of God, he is separated, vulnerable, and alone making him an easy target.

God's love factors that we are one with God, not divided from Him. Unity with God is the message of the Gospel of peace, which shods our feet in battle - Ephesians 6:15. When feet are protected with the conviction that we are loved by God in a great way, we are established to dig into battle in prayer. We will not be moved by the machination of the atmosphere and circumstances that endeavor to sway and subdue us, the victorious believers, in prayer.

"Thou greatly beloved"!

DAY 26
NO DISTANCE IN PRAYER

Fear not, Daniel: for from the first day that thou didst set thine heart to understand, and to chasten thyself before thy God, thy words were heard, and I am come for thy words. But the prince of the kingdom of Persia withstood me one and twenty days: but, lo, Michael, one of the chief princes, came to help me; and I remained there with the kings of Persia. - Daniel 10:12-13

"If thou art running to Christ, He is already near thee. If thou dost sigh for His presence, that sigh is the evidence that He is with thee. He is with thee now: therefore be calmly glad." - Charles Spurgeon

It is of great comfort to read the words penned "from the first day...thy words were heard, and I am come for thy words." Be glad child of God for our words are heard "from the first day"! This should cheer the wavering saint who labors in prayer!

When we think of international communication and how back in the day it used to take weeks to have a painstakingly written letter delivered to it's eagerly awaiting addressee, we can truly appreciate the fact that there is no distance between the seeking soul and the listening God. We tend to think of God naturally, in terms of distance, that He is far away in the heavens on a throne, but nothing could be farther from the truth.

In the sphere of prayer there is no distance, no interference, no walls, no obstacle to catch our rising prayer and cast it to the ground. God is closer to the believer than the believer is to himself. As a matter of a fact, before we pray He knows our prayer altogether - Psalm139:4.

In warfare it is critical to know that there is no distance that our prayer must travel. A whisper of a prayer can be more powerful than a prayer of shouting and pleading with God. Often due to a delay of the answer, we assume there is distance, but contrary to appearance, He instantly hears and He instantly acts.

Yet there are times of a hindering of the execution of that prayer as we see in Daniel's case. Though Daniel did not immediately know of the delay of an answer due to warfare and hindering, Daniel continued to fast and pray. It is of utmost importance that we cease not in prayer, that we knock until the door is opened. Because the answer is coming and your constancy in prayer is part of the warfare being waged. All too often answers to prayers in transit are halted due to the breakdown of prayer.

When a person begins to discover the power of prayer, the Prince of Persia, the unseen authority of Ephesians 6:12, will begin his hindering program. He will use feelings, pressure, circumstances, people, or personal distractions to get the praying warrior to stumble in his prayer and stop. He will project impulses, fears, bad news, or whatever he can send to stop the prayers.

Were Daniel's prayers a part of the victory in that Michael the Angel was sent to help get the words to Daniel of the vision? I think so. For when we read the disciple's prayer of Matthew 6 we read "Thy will be done on earth as it is in heaven." The distance between the will of Heaven and the will of God accomplished on the earth is only a prayer away. When we pray, God's will is accomplished. When we abide in prayer, we are an acting agent, an ambassador, that becomes a conduit of the accomplishment of the things of God on this earth.

We must remember that the devil is the "Prince of the Power of the Air" so he has authority in the air, but not absolute authority. When believers live in their flesh, in the wisdom of this world, they become conduits of the air giving place for the devil, even speaking his mind about God's people and God's work. That is why when we are Spirit-filled we can detect demonic activity when we enter certain locales of entertainment, carnal activity, or territories given over to sin.

Be ever aware of the words that you speak and what you put out into the air. Negativity and fear, carnal comments, natural deductions, and personal opinions devoid of truth actually give the devil a stronghold to traffic in the air causing pressure and oppression over people.

It can be clearly observed when we travel to certain countries, and cities that are ruled by corrupt Godless political leaders, how the atmosphere of the country is heavy and oppressed. It is a great joy that when we pray, the atmosphere in which the Prince of the Power of the Air dwells, cannot stop or slow our prayers. Actually when we pray, the atmosphere is confronted and is cleared. Nothing was more effective in clearing the air in the Bible than the spoken Word of God and the prayer of the saints. Just as the air in a lightning storm is ionized and purged, so is the thick atmosphere of Satanic activity in warfare when the prayers of you and me arise

DAY 27
PRINCE OF THE POWER OF THE AIR

"Wherein in time past ye walked according to the course of this world, according to the prince of the power of the air, the spirit that now worketh in the children of disobedience" - Ephesians 2:2

"Satan dreads nothing but prayer. His one concern is to keep the saints from praying. He fears nothing from prayerless studies, prayerless work, prayerless religion. He laughs at our toil, he mocks our wisdom, but he trembles when we pray." - Samuel Chadwick

It is evident that prayer uttered takes place in the air, in the invisible sphere of the atmosphere around us. It is in this spatial environment we call "air" that the Prince of the Power of the Air vies for position and causes pressure. That is why Satanic attacks on the saint are always accompanied by "pressure" and "oppression." The word Paul used in Ephesians 2;2 for "air" is the greek word aer which differed from the word aither. Aither or ether for the Greeks was a higher, purer air that was clear and without substance or congestion. Aer, which Paul uses in Ephesians 2:2, is a word to describe the space between the Earth and the universe, in other words, our atmosphere. This aer was in contrast to aither for the Greeks in that it was not clear or pure air, but it was thick and cloudy, the sphere where much traffic took place. Paul the Apostle, very astutely pinpointed the territory of the Prince of the Power of the Air as aer - thick, cloudy, and full of demonic traffic.

Physics tells us that there are various frequencies that are carried through the air we habitate in. Sparing the verbose explanation of radio waves, the behavior of short-wave, long-wave, and ultra-micro waves and their affect on the human body, there is a valid argument that as human beings, we are subject to a wide spectrum of frequencies that impact us and our state of being. During the Cold War years, the Americans and Russians experimented much with the effect of low-wave as well as high-frequency waves on weather, earthquakes, and people's moods and behavior. It is curious, to say the least, that the results of these tests and their effects are highly classified even to this day.

So we are in no wise taken by surprise that the prince of the aer uses the medium of the air as a highway for

his congested demonic traffic and invisible projections. "Satanic projection" is a term that we use to describe the process of Satan, "the Father of all lies" - John 8:44, in which he creates a lie, then broadcasts it through the air to any person "tuned" to believe that particular lie. Just as a radio, or a device has a digital address, it is tuned to a set frequency for the purpose of receiving, decoding, and assimilating specific information sent by broadcast. This demonic traffic is described in Ezekiel 28:5. "By your great wisdom and by your traffic you have increased your riches and power, and your heart is proud and lifted up because of your wealth."

This concept can be illustrated in what Jesus said in John 8:44, that "Ye are of your father the devil, and the lusts of your father ye will do." The accusers of Jesus could not hear or understand what Jesus was saying because they were tuned to what their lusts were set on and thus they heard only the broadcast of their father the devil, which at that moment was saying in the setting of that chapter, "Murder Jesus."

Another illustration of this phenomenon is the Blackpoll Warbler. This little bird weighs only three-quarters of an ounce! Yet in the fall it can travel from Alaska to New England, flying thousands of miles yearly to the same exact location to mate. When the cold comes, the tiny bird heads to South America via Africa, a combined total of 2,400 miles! Out over the Atlantic Ocean it flies at an altitude of up to 20,000 feet in the air. The bird, weighing only ounces, has an antenna that is tuned to a sonic location that the earth

and nature are broadcasting on the magnetic plane. According to the U.S.G.S., the earth emits vibrations and frequencies that are like a compass or a GPS. This
is the signal the Blackpoll Warbler follows until it is safely at its destination.

The human being also has an antenna that processes thousands of vibrations and signals every second. This is no mystery; it is the organ called the hypothalamus. The hypothalamus is not a gland, but it is attached to the pineal gland. It is a bundle of fibers, nerves, and blood vessels emanating from the thalamus that handles the main output of the limbic system. The limbic system is basic to motivation, emotion, and reward processes in the brain. The hypothalamus is particularly important for maintaining homeostasis, the proper balance of the body's internal environment. Without being unwarrantedly technical, the hypothalamus, when stimulated (observed by Steinbaum & Miller - 1965 and Teitelbaum & Epstein - 1962) can trigger aggression indicating anger and/or fear, and many other functions related to motivation and emotion. Thus the projections of the Prince of the Power of the Air are broadcasted to the mind that is invariably tuned to the lusts of the flesh. These projections hone into the fleshly mind with the intent that those vibrations translate into thoughts, feelings, and eventually, actions.

The devil projects lies in James 3:15. These atmospheric projections are constrained to an earthly gravitational pull downward and self-ward. This can be the case for the Christian. He may allow a place marked off for the devil in his soul - Ephesians 4:27

and because it has not been taken to the Cross, that area becomes a magnet for projections, subjectivity, and egotism. Satanic projections may only have power and leverage when they find the soft tissue of uncrucified flesh.

There is a Biblical account of this very thing happening in Psalm 106:15. "And He gave them their request, but sent leanness into their souls and [thinned their numbers by] disease and death." (Amplified) When fleshly desire and petitions do not pass through death at the Cross, they infect our prayers causing us to "ask amiss" - James 4:3. Due to the law of attraction, God may very well allow us to have the request that we petition for if we insist on having it. But this will only be for our undoing.

Nevertheless, the Cross is the great interrupter of the processes of projections. For at the Cross, another law takes over delivering us from the law of sin and death, the law of the spirit of life in Romans 8:4.

Prayer and the Word deliver us to the Cross that frees us from projections in the aer and tune us in to the mind of Christ. Then we may begin to hear from God in prayer in the midst of spiritual warfare.

DAY 28
PROJECTIONS IN THE AIR

"Then cometh Jesus with them unto a place called Gethsemane, and saith unto the disciples, Sit ye here, while I go and pray yonder. And he took with him Peter and the two sons of Zebedee, and began to be sorrowful and very heavy. Then saith he unto them, My soul is exceeding sorrowful, even unto death:tarry ye here, and watch with me. And he went a little further, and fell on his face, and prayed, saying, O my Father, if it be possible, let this cup pass from me:nevertheless not as I will, but as thou wilt. And he cometh unto the disciples, and findeth them asleep, and saith unto Peter, What, could ye not watch with me one hour? Watch and pray, that ye enter not into temptation:the spirit indeed is willing, but the flesh is weak. He went away again the second time, and prayed, saying, O my Father, if this cup may not pass away from me, except I drink it, thy will be done. And he came and found them asleep again:for their eyes were heavy." - Matthew 26:36-43

"Another part or piece,' said Diabolus, 'of mine excellent armour, is a dumb and prayerless spirit, a spirit that scorns to cry for mercy, let the danger be ever so great; therefore be you, my Mansoul, sure that you make use of this." — John Bunyan, The Holy War

In light of yesterday's meditation, we see clearly the once hidden medium of the Adversary's highway of trafficking. No longer may we be ignorant of the methodia - 2 Corinthians 2:11 of the devil that aims to beguile and render passive the most powerful weapon of the believer - prayer.

Yet that old serpent does not cease to project his fiery darts at the saint's shield of faith and armor of light, in hopes of breaking through the impenetrable by a small crack or tear due to a place marked for him in the flesh - Ephesians 4:27. If the Devil cannot win in our decision making, our determination, or our affections and commitment, he most assuredly targets our physical body and it's chemistry via the medium of the air of Ephesians 2:2. He will send a thought or impulse through the air to the antennae of the body, the hypothalamus, if the Mind of Christ is not dominant in our lives - Philippians 2:5 & 1 Corinthians 2:16. The Mind of Christ instructs the believer in real time to discern projections that exalt themselves above the knowledge of the present Lord - 2 Corinthians 10:5. "Casting down imaginations, and every high thing that exalteth itself against the knowledge of God, and bringing into captivity every thought to the obedience of Christ.

The word "imaginations" here in this verse, in the original Greek is logizomai, which when translated to the English gives us the word we use "projections." Logizomai, are well thought out calculations, reckonings, considerations, and counsel from the Evil One with its cross-hairs on the believer's old sin nature, or fallen flesh. Any area of the believer's life that is not surrendered to the Cross of Christ and under the authority of God's hand is an area that can be penetrated and infected by logizomai. These projections are fiery by nature in that they burn from the inside out. Invisible projections penetrate; and when not checked by the precise Word of God, they will hijack the believer's decision making and self-consciousness with the purpose of acting out the counsels (dialogízomai) of Hell - Proverbs 6:18 (Septuagint).

We see this with Peter in Matthew 16 when he, in seeming sentimental care, forbade Jesus to speak of going to the Cross to finish the work; hence Jesus' harsh rebuke "get thee behind me Satan." When you and I are not being quickened moment by moment in the Holy Spirit recall of the Word of Grace, we are candidates to be mouthpieces for the atmosphere. In other words, The Prince of the Power of the Air did not want Jesus going to the cross. As a result, he projected to Peter his satanic counsel to hinder Jesus from carrying out His Mission by targeting Peter's area of sentimentality, which was unguarded by the Word. When the projection made it's way to the area marked off for the Devil in Ephesians 4:27, the counsels of Hell took over Peter's mouth momentarily and he spoke forbidding Jesus. Jesus acutely discerned the whole process and addressed the projection and its source - Satan.

How does this relate to prayer and warfare? Most applicably!
What was Jesus' request to the disciples? "Watch with me one hour." Oh! and that is all He asks from you and me today. To watch with Him in prayer! For as we watch, we discern and we wage proper warfare in casting down imaginations and projections in the arena of a seemingly pacific green garden we call Earth.

One more word on this subject of projections; when Paul used the phrase "casting down" he was using a word combination in the Greek that alluded to what rulers and kings do when there is another potentate or prince rising to power to challenge authority. It means to literally "tear down with finality from top to bottom." Any counsel or thought process that rises its proud head above the Mind of Christ we "tear down" in entirety through the authority we have as "sons of God" - John 1:12, so to never rise again.

In our opening Scripture we read of Peter's sluggishness and slumber in the Garden of Gethsemane while Jesus was subject to demonic guerrilla warfare in the air. Why was Peter so sluggish as well as the other disciples? It was because the traffic in the air was so thick and dense with demonic activity that their physical bodies became so dull to the activity of the Spirit that they slept. The Spirit was "willing" to quicken their mortal, physical bodies, as in Romans 8:11, but alas, they, like us, did not watch.

When we are sober-minded, being quickened by the Spirit, we are keen to discern with understanding, spiritual warfare - Isaiah 11:3. Most Christians are ignorant of spiritual warfare, and have no idea of atmospheric traffic. They would have put this little book aside a long time ago and resolved to live in their small world of circumstances, skirmishes, and petty battles that have nothing to do with their true victory in Christ and ruling in their life. They shall have their portion in this life and leanness of soul - Psalm 106:15.

To "wage a good warfare" as Paul spoke of, there must be insight, understanding, and discernment from the Word of God, detecting the movements of the Enemy many miles, and many years ahead of time, before the projection is even determined in the mind of the Hinderer.

DAY 29
PRAYER VERSUS THE LAW OF ATTRACTION

"But the hour cometh, and now is, when the true worshippers shall worship the Father in spirit and in truth:for the Father -- seeketh such to worship him. God is a Spirit:and they that worship him must worship him in spirit and in truth." - John 4:23-24

"I have lived to thank God that not all my prayers have been answered." - Jean Ingelow

Because of the deep nature of prayer there is the mystical aspect to it since prayer comes from the depths of a person. But let us not be naive; a pagan can pray as ardently as a saint. The Hindu or Muslim may pray with great dedication focusing his petition toward his god. The satanist prays to his demon as well as the loyal sports fan who hopes with all his heart and all his lucky charms that his team will win. We have also seen and heard of these forceful prayers having a profound and supernatural effect on the outcome of the desired thing. This is no more than the universal law of attraction that Rumi, the Persian mystic sufist wrote of in the 13th century, "That which you seek, seeks you."

Many deceptive books can be found about this illustrious subject on the law of attraction. This law can be exemplified by the notion that when two or more people passionately desire the same thing, they will always find each other, even though they reside on opposite ends of the world. It can also be seen in the phenomenon of a person with earnest desire or need and the very object, opportunity, or relationship they want finds them.

Overall, the subject of the inert fallen power laying dormant in the human soul has been little discussed in Christianity, thus in the ignorance of its existence, the devil has been free to utilize its force in religion to counterfeit true prayer and worship. Thus let us briefly discuss it today.

Physicians say that 80% or more of the human brain appears to be unused. Mesmer, in his controversial psychic experiments in 1778 confirmed that within an individual, there is a soul-force that can be developed and expressed either in a physical or religious setting. We call this "soul-power." When Adam fell, many of the miraculous abilities in his soul that he had been endowed with by God became entrapped, confined, and hidden in the flesh, latent.

Since the fall of Adam, Satan has been striving to redevelop that part of man that lays dormant in his soul. He wants to remake man into a new being that knows intuitively his world and universe, being harmoniously one with it. He wants to remodel man into what he was before the fall, only with the exception that he is not in communion with God, but under the dominion of the god of this world. Satan lost his dominion over this world when he fell and became inferior to Adam's God-given authority. Today the devil wants to control man and his soul-power to create a utopia without God. This happens to be the shared goal and vision of the New Age movement and the main stream political trend.

In every aspect of this cosmic world system, Satan wants to replace God with himself and take the place of the Trinity in every facet of its work. It should be of no surprise that many miracles in the world today, and even in the church, may not be of the Spirit of God but of the soul that has become skilled in its abilities. While living in Ukraine in the early 90's, I saw first-hand people that had the soul ability to heal little children and cast spells and they were not even saved.

To attain his goal, the devil has to "be as the Most High" and to make men "as gods." He wants to break down the shell and hedge around every person through the corruption in the world - 2 Peter 1:4. Satan does this through man's inherent nature of lust, which releases the soul-power within, resulting in lawless living. In doing so, he eventually aims to create the perfect man, the man that will be known as the "anti-christ" who will have perfected his soul-power and have abilities that Paul describes in 2 Thessalonians 2:9 as "lying wonders."

The Great Counterfeiter wants the believer to be ignorant of the fact that prayer and warfare in prayer does not take place in the sphere of the soul of the believer, nor is prayer a force of the soul. Though individuals or groups of people have used their soul-power directed at an event or individual and have actually influenced the outcome; this is not how the mystery of spiritual prayer works.

Prayer for the child of God is not a force tainted by the corruption of soul-power because prayer takes place in the Truth and the Spirit of God - John 4:23-24. True warfare in prayer cannot be waged using the power of the soul through concentration, focus, personal development, or physical neglect. Warfare in prayer takes its place from the platform of the spirit which we will address in the next chapter.

DAY 30
SOULISH PRAYER

"Verily, verily, I say unto you, Except a grain of wheat fall into the earth and die, it abideth by itself alone; but if it die, it beareth much fruit. He that loveth his life loseth it; and he that hateth his life in this world shall keep it unto life eternal" (John 12:24,25)

"Men may spurn our appeals, reject our message, oppose our arguments, despise our persons, but they are helpless against our prayers." - J. Sidlow Baxter

Due to the fact that the human soul is bound in self-consciousness, the sacred act of prayer cannot take place in the soul. For the soul, in its own boundaries, cannot see beyond itself, know beyond its own understanding, and cannot worship anyone else other than its own preferences. As we spoke of earlier in this devotional, people confuse spiritual experiences with rare, deep feelings they have experienced that take place in their soul. What many call spiritual events in their life may actually be only soulish at best. The majority of people live in the realm of their flesh and physical stimulation to the point that when feeling and power arise from their soul, they mistake it for spirituality naming it a "powerful experience."

Some well known preachers and healers of present utilize their soul-power as a force in their meetings via hypnotic techniques where attendees have actually experienced healings and various forms of embetterment. Yet it has been documented that many of those relieved of their symptoms by the forces of soulish prayers have only had their ailment come back in greater measure to torment them even more - Matthew 12:44.

Though the soul may have two separate abilities, (one to know itself and another to perform powerful wonders) the soul is always bound to itself and thus what it is able to achieve is never eternal and everlasting, but temporal. Prayer that takes place only in the soul is prayer that prays to itself - Luke 18:11, prays according to its own ability and answers its own prayers. Prayer in the soul is not supernatural, though it may appear powerful.

Soul-power and force from a individual's persona is always characterized by the presence of pressure and oppression. The flesh and the soul broadcast vibrations that are tuned to their own desires and lust patterns - Mark 7:21-23, with a pull inward and self-ward. A discerning person can feel it in a meeting or conversation. This always leads to spiritual bondage because the soul is bound to itself, and its self-consiousness, though it seeks freedom. Soulish people are manipulative and so are their prayers - John 11:32. Service for God and prayer that is soulish is always bound to earthliness - James 3:15, and always makes circumstances, people, and self the issue. When people function in their soul-force, there is no joy in their prayer, in their service, or in themselves.

Paul served God in the realm of his spirit - Romans 1:9, not in his soul, hence his anointing and powerful, freeing ministry of the Gospel. Paul did not wage war by his soul because the weapons of his warfare were not carnal but spiritual - 2 Corinthians 10:4, to the effect of pulling down satanic strongholds. Satanic strongholds do not dwell in a person's physical body but in their soul. Too many make the issue of the health of their physical body when the issue truly lays in the structure of their soul and what dwells hidden there.

The soul-life seeks to be stronger and so does soulish Christianity. God is not seeking stronger prayer warriors but believers that have a deeper deprivation from their intoxicating soul-power. The key to effective spiritual prayer in warfare is not more power but more death to self and soul-power.

In John 12:24, 25 lies the ultimate key to all aspects of spirituality. It is the breaking and death of the shell, the vessel, the soul-life. In the Greek it reads "He that loves his soul-life loses it." Self-love is the great cancer today in the Church. "He that hateth his soul-life in this cosmic world order shall keep it..."

Hatred for the soul-life is not as the religious sadomasochists define it, as beating and destroying their evil physical bodies. The body is not the shell that needs to be broken, it is the soul which needs to be brought into subjection. True freedom and power comes rather by delivering up our soul-life and all its force and power to the Cross of Calvary - that Great Resolution. For it is the love for the Cross and its Champion Jesus that causes us to hate whatever is in its way. The Cross obliterates anything else other than the exaltation of Jesus Christ and the will of the Father.

We wage an effective warfare in prayer in the Spirit when the soul and its force have been stilled in God's presence. Then the soul finds its peace, its joy, and the freedom it seeks - Habakkuk 2:20.

CONCLUSION
The Place and Outpouring of Prayer

"Praying always with all prayer and supplication in the Spirit, and watching thereunto with all perseverance and supplication for all saints; And for me, that utterance may be given unto me, that I may open my mouth boldly, to make known the mystery of the gospel." -Ephesians 6:18-19

The fountain of prayer and all supplications is sourced in the limitless flow of the Holy Spirit who knows the "deep things of God" - 2 Corinthians 2:10. The Spirit reveals those deep and secret things hidden in the darkness, Daniel 2:22, dark not because some evil or horror dwells there, but dark due to the ignorance of many to its riches.

Prayer sourced in the Spirit is true worship - John 4:23. It has been weaned from the obstructions of sight and the tantrums of the restless soul. It is prayer that rises above the opaque columnous clouds, above the cyclic rise and fall of the worldly fray, above the frivolous opining of men and far above the frenetic traffic of the "Prince of the Power of the Air".

When we have entered into the Holiest of Holies, having passed through the outer court of the world and the flesh, passing through the veil by the Cross of Jesus Christ, we discover that meager ability of the soul is too incompetent to comprehend what awaits the believer at the Throne of Grace. Only the prayer whose path was made by our Hero, Jesus Christ the Forerunner, can bring us there.

That Holiest Place is the altar where the atoning Blood has been applied. There is true freedom from the bonds of the corrupt nature of the flesh and the chains of the self-consciousness of the human soul. That Holiest Place is the sphere of the Spirit, where we hear the voice of the Word of God speaking to the deepest parts of us, seeing us, knowing us, and counseling us.

The "Mystery of the Gospel" of which Paul spoke is not an esoteric mystery that cannot be known, it is this very thing - the mystery of knowing the depths of God: His Mind, His Plan, and His Grace. All these await the believer in the Word and in prayer. When we have been alone with Him in prayer and have opened our mouths in prayer, there in secret, we will observe that the Witness of God accompanies us as we preach the Gospel. Prayer sourced in the Spirit always guides us to the Gospel of Christ. Prayer's ultimate heartbeat is to bring the lost sinner into communion with God and his new creation in Christ.

Prayer without the Gospel is not prayer. Prayer and preaching are married and undivorceable. One cannot be without the other without both ceasing to exist. For when we find ourselves in the midst of His

Holiest, time will not tarry long before we hear "Who will go for us?" - Isaiah 6:1-8

Prayer instills the mystery of a power in us that did not exist there before. It gives us hunger for holiness, missions, service, compassion, and the desire to serve.

Let our knees be marked with the inscriptions of our floors, let our lips be filled with His Praise, let our souls be stilled in His presence, let our heart burn with the matters of the Lord, and let our minds mull the burdens of the Lord . Let us be those men and women that have the marks of our Savior, that we too may be known as "those that had been with Jesus." For God knows this dying world desperately needs it.

"There is a place where thou canst touch the eyes
Of blinded men to instant, perfect sight;
There is a place where thou canst say, "Arise"
To dying captives, bound in chains of night;
There is a place where thou canst reach the store
Of hoarded gold and free it for the Lord;
There is a place—upon some distant shore—
Where thou canst send the worker and the Word.
Where is that secret place—dost thou ask, "Where?"
O soul, it is the secret place of prayer!"
~ Alfred Lord Tennyson

This small treatise on prayer has come to a close, but the start of an earth shaking era of prayer is just beginning.

FINIS

To Read More Books & Articles by this Author
Please Visit:
www.Goye4th.org